My Beautiful Laundrette
and
The Rainbow Sign

HANIF KUREISHI

ff

faber and faber

LONDON · BOSTON

First published in 1986
by Faber and Faber Limited
3 Queen Square London WC1N 3AU
Reprinted in 1986

Photoset by Wilmaset Birkenhead Merseyside
Printed in Great Britain by
Redwood Burn Ltd Trowbridge Wiltshire
All rights reserved

British Library Cataloguing in Publication Data

Kureishi, Hanif
My beautiful laundrette
I. Title
822'.914   PR6061.U7/

ISBN 0-571-13981-7

Contents

The Rainbow Sign   7
Introduction to *My Beautiful Laundrette*   39
My Beautiful Laundrette   45

The Rainbow Sign

'God gave Noah the rainbow sign,
No more water, the fire next time!'

One: England

I was born in London of an English mother and Pakistani father. My father, who lives in London, came to England from Bombay in 1947 to be educated by the old colonial power. He married here and never went back to India. The rest of his large family, his brothers, their wives, his sisters, moved from Bombay to Karachi, in Pakistan, after partition.

Frequently during my childhood, I met my Pakistani uncles when they came to London on business. They were important, confident people who took me to hotels, restaurants and Test matches, often in taxis. But I had no idea of what the sub-continent was like or how my numerous uncles, aunts and cousins lived there. When I was nine or ten a teacher purposefully placed some pictures of Indian peasants in mud huts in front of me and said to the class: Hanif comes from India. I wondered: did my uncles ride on camels? Surely not in their suits? Did my cousins, so like me in other ways, squat down in the sand like little Mowglis, half-naked and eating with their fingers?

In the mid-1960s, Pakistanis were a risible subject in England, derided on television and exploited by politicians. They had the worst jobs, they were uncomfortable in England, some of them had difficulties with the language. They were despised and out of place.

From the start I tried to deny my Pakistani self. I was ashamed. It was a curse and I wanted to be rid of it. I wanted to be like everyone else. I read with understanding a story in a newspaper about a black boy who, when he noticed that burnt skin turned white, jumped into a bath of boiling water.

At school, one teacher always spoke to me in a 'Peter Sellers' Indian accent. Another refused to call me by my name, calling me Pakistani Pete instead. So I refused to call the teacher by *his* name and used his nickname instead. This led to trouble; arguments, detentions, escapes from school over hedges, and eventually suspension. This played into my hands; this couldn't have been better.

With a friend I roamed the streets and fields all day; I sat beside streams; I stole yellow lurex trousers from a shop and smuggled them out of the house under my school trousers; I hid in woods reading hard books; and I saw the film *Zulu* several times.

This friend, who became Johnny in my film, *My Beautiful Laundrette*, came one day to the house. It was a shock.

He was dressed in jeans so tough they almost stood up by themselves. These were suspended above his boots by Union Jack braces of 'hangman's strength', revealing a stretch of milk bottle white leg. He seemed to have sprung up several inches because of his Doctor Marten's boots, which had steel caps and soles as thick as cheese sandwiches. His Ben Sherman shirt with a pleat down the back was essential. And his hair, which was only a quarter of an inch long all over, stuck out of his head like little nails. This unmoving creation he concentratedly touched up every hour with a sharpened steel comb that also served as a dagger.

He soon got the name Bog Brush, though this was not a moniker you would use to his face. Where before he was an angel-boy with a blond quiff flattened down by his mother's loving spit, a clean handkerchief always in his pocket, as well as being a keen cornet player for the Air Cadets he'd now gained a brand-new truculent demeanour.

My mother was so terrified by this stormtrooper dancing on her doorstep to the 'Skinhead Moonstomp', which he moaned to himself continuously, that she had to lie down.

I decided to go out roaming with B.B. before my father got home from work. But it wasn't the same as before. We couldn't have our talks without being interrupted. Bog Brush had become Someone. To his intense pleasure, similarly-dressed strangers greeted Bog Brush in the street as if they were in a war-torn foreign country and in the same army battalion. We were suddenly banned from cinemas. The Wimpy Bar in which we sat for hours with milkshakes wouldn't let us in. As a matter of pride we now had to go round the back and lob a brick at the rear window of the place.

Other strangers would spot us from the other side of the street. B.B. would yell 'Leg it!' as the enemy dashed through traffic and leapt over the bonnets of cars to get at us, screaming obscenities and chasing us up alleys, across allotments, around reservoirs, and on and on.

And then, in the evening, B.B. took me to meet with the other lads. We climbed the park railings and strolled across to the football pitch, by the goal posts. This is where the lads congregated to hunt down Pakistanis and beat them. Most of them I was at school with. The others I'd grown up with. I knew their parents. They knew my father.

I withdrew, from the park, from the lads, to a safer place, within myself. I moved into what I call my 'temporary' period. I was only waiting now to get away, to leave the London suburbs, to make another kind of life, somewhere else, with better people.

In this isolation, in my bedroom where I listened to the Pink Floyd, the Beatles and the John Peel Show, I started to write down the speeches of politicians, the words which helped create the neo-Nazi attitudes I saw around me. This I called 'keeping the accounts'.

In 1965, Enoch Powell said: 'We should not lose sight of the desirability of achieving a steady flow of voluntary repatriation for the elements which are proving unsuccessful or unassimilable.'

In 1967, Duncan Sandys said: 'The breeding of millions of half-caste children would merely produce a generation of misfits and create national tensions.'

I wasn't a misfit; I could join the elements of myself together. It was the others, they wanted misfits; they wanted you to embody within yourself their ambivalence.

Also in 1967, Enoch Powell – who once said he would love to have been Viceroy of India – quoted a constituent of his as saying that because of the Pakistanis 'this country will not be worth living in for our children'.

And Powell said, more famously: 'As I look ahead I am filled with foreboding. Like the Roman, "I seem to see the River Tiber foaming with much blood".'

As Powell's speeches appeared in the papers, graffiti in support of him appeared in the London streets. Racists gained confidence. People insulted me in the street. Someone in a café refused to eat at the same table with me. The parents of a girl I was in love with told her she'd get a bad reputation by going out with darkies.

Powell allowed himself to become a figurehead for racists. He helped create racism in Britain and was directly responsible not only for the atmosphere of fear and hatred, but through his influence, for individual acts of violence against Pakistanis.

Television comics used Pakistanis as the butt of their humour. Their jokes were highly political: they contributed to a way of seeing the world. The enjoyed reduction of racial hatred to a joke did two things: it expressed a collective view (which was sanctioned by its being on the BBC), and it was a celebration of contempt in millions of living rooms in England. I was afraid to watch TV because of it; it was too embarrassing, too degrading.

Parents of my friends, both lower-middle-class and working-class, often told me they were Powell supporters. Sometimes I heard them talking, heatedly, violently, about race, about 'the Pakis'. I was desperately embarrassed and afraid of being identified with these loathed aliens. I found it almost impossible to answer questions about where I came from. The word 'Pakistani' had been made into an insult. It was a word I didn't want used about myself. I couldn't tolerate being myself.

The British complained incessantly that the Pakistanis wouldn't assimilate. This meant they wanted the Pakistanis to be exactly like them. But of course even then they would have rejected them.

The British were doing the assimilating: they assimilated Pakistanis to their world view. They saw them as dirty, ignorant and less than human – worthy of abuse and violence.

At this time I found it difficult to get along with anyone. I was frightened and hostile. I suspected that my white friends were capable of racist insults. And many of them did taunt me, innocently. I reckoned that at least once every day since I was five years old I had been racially abused. I became incapable of distinguishing between remarks that were genuinely intended to hurt and those intended as 'humour'.

I became cold and distant. I began to feel I was very violent. But I didn't know how to be violent. If I had known, if that had come naturally to me, or if there'd been others I could follow, I would have made my constant fantasies of revenge into realities, I would have got into trouble, willingly hurt people, or set fire to things.

But I mooched around libraries. There, in an old copy of *Life* magazine, I found pictures of the Black Panthers. It was Eldridge Cleaver, Huey Newton, Bobby Seale and their confederates in black vests and slacks, with Jimi Hendrix haircuts. Some of them were holding guns, the Army .45 and the 12-gauge Magnum shotgun with 18-inch barrel that Huey specified for street fighting.

I tore down my pictures of the Rolling Stones and Cream and replaced them with the Panthers. I found it all exhilarating. These people were proud and they were fighting. To my knowledge, no one in England was fighting.

There was another, more important picture.

On the cover of the Penguin edition of *The Fire Next Time*, was James Baldwin holding a child, his nephew. Baldwin, having suffered, having been there, was all anger and understanding. He was intelligence and love combined. As I planned my escape I read Baldwin all the time, I read Richard Wright and I admired Muhammad Ali.

A great moment occurred when I was in a sweet shop. I saw through to a TV in the backroom on which was showing the 1968 Olympic Games in Mexico. Thommie Smith and John Carlos were raising their fists on the victory rostrum, giving the Black Power salute as the 'Star Spangled Banner' played. The white shopkeeper was outraged. He said to me: they shouldn't mix politics and sport.

During this time there was always Muhammad Ali, the former Cassius Clay, a great sportsman become black spokesman. Now a Muslim, millions of fellow Muslims all over the world prayed for his victory when he fought.

And there was the Nation of Islam movement to which Ali belonged, led by the man who called himself the Messenger of Islam and wore a gold-embroidered fez, Elijah Muhammad.

Elijah was saying in the mid-1960s that the rule of the white devils would end in fifteen years. He preached separatism, separate development for black and white. He ran his organization by charisma and threat, claiming that anyone who challenged him would be chastened by Allah. Apparently Allah also turned the minds of defectors into a turmoil.

Elijah's disciple Malcolm X, admirer of Gandhi and self-confirmed anti-Semite, accepted in prison that 'the key to a Muslim is submission, the attunement of one towards Allah'. That this glorious resistance to the white man, the dismissal of Christian meekness, was followed by submission to Allah and worse, to Elijah Muhammad, was difficult to take.

I saw racism as unreason and prejudice, ignorance and a failure of sense; it was Fanon's 'incomprehension'. That the men I wanted to admire had liberated themselves only to take to unreason, to the abdication of intelligence, was shocking to me. And the separatism, the total loathing of the white man as innately corrupt, the 'All whites are devils' view, was equally unacceptable. I had to live in England, in the suburbs of London, with whites. My mother was white. I wasn't ready for separate development. I'd had too much of that already.

Luckily James Baldwin wasn't too keen either. In *The Fire Next Time* he describes a visit to Elijah Muhammad. He tells of how close he feels to Elijah and how he wishes to be able to love him. But when he tells Elijah that he has many white friends, he receives Elijah's pity. For Elijah the whites' time is up. It's no good Baldwin telling him he has white friends with whom he'd entrust his life.

As the evening goes on, Baldwin tires of the sycophancy around Elijah. He and Elijah would always be strangers and 'possibly enemies'. Baldwin deplores the black Muslims' turning to Africa and to Islam, this turning away from the reality of America and 'inventing' the past. Baldwin also mentions Malcolm X and the chief of the American Nazi party saying that racially speaking they were in complete agreement: they both wanted separate development. Baldwin adds that the debasement of one race and the glorification of another in this way inevitably leads to murder.

After this the Muslims weren't too keen on Baldwin, to say the least. Eldridge Cleaver, who once raped white women 'on principle', had a picture of Elijah Muhammad, the great strength-giver, on his prison wall. Later he became a devoted supporter of Malcolm X.

Cleaver says of Baldwin: 'There is in James Baldwin's work the most gruelling, agonizing, total hatred of the blacks, particularly of himself, and the most shameful, fanatical, fawning, sycophantic love of the whites that one can find in the writing of any black American writer of note in our time.'

How strange it was to me, this worthless abuse of a writer who could enter the minds and skins of both black and white, and the good just anger turning to passionate Islam as a source of pride instead of to a digested political commitment to a different kind of whole society. And this easy thrilling talk of 'white devils' instead of close analysis of the institutions that kept blacks low.

I saw the taking up of Islam as an aberration, a desperate fantasy of world-wide black brotherhood; it was a symptom of extreme alienation. It was also an inability to seek a wider political view or cooperation with other oppressed groups – or with the working class as a whole – since alliance with white groups was necessarily out of the question.

I had no idea what an Islamic society would be like, what the application of the authoritarian theology Elijah preached would mean in practice. I forgot about it, fled the suburbs, went to university, got started as a writer and worked as an usher at the Royal Court Theatre. It was over ten years before I went to an Islamic country.

Two: Pakistan

The man had heard that I was interested in talking about his country, Pakistan, and that this was my first visit. He kindly kept trying to take me aside to talk. But I was already being talked to.

I was at another Karachi party, in a huge house, with a glass of whisky in one hand, and a paper plate in the other. Casually I'd mentioned to a woman friend of the family that I wasn't against marriage. Now this friend was earnestly recommending to me a young woman who wanted to move to Britain, with a husband. To my discomfort this go-between was trying to fix a time for the three of us to meet and negotiate.

I went to three parties a week in Karachi. This time, when I could get away from this woman, I was with landowners, diplomats, businessmen and politicians: powerful people. This pleased me. They were people I wouldn't have been able to get to in England and I wanted to write about them.

They were drinking heavily. Every liberal in England knows you can be lashed for drinking in Pakistan. But as far as I could tell, none of this English-speaking international bourgeoisie would be lashed for anything. They all had their favourite trusted bootleggers who negotiated the potholes of Karachi at high speed on disintegrating motorcycles, with the hooch stashed on the back. Bad bootleggers passed a hot needle through the neck of your bottle and drew your whisky out. Stories were told of guests politely sipping ginger beer with their ice and soda, glancing at other guests to see if they were drunk and wondering if their own alcohol tolerance had miraculously increased.

I once walked into a host's bathroom to see the bath full of floating whisky bottles being soaked to remove the labels, a servant sitting on a stool serenely poking at them with a stick.

So it was all as tricky and expensive as buying cocaine in London, with the advantage that as the hooch market was so competitive, the 'leggers delivered video tapes at the same time, dashing into the room towards the TV with hot copies of *The Jewel In The Crown*, *The Far Pavilions*, and an especially popular programme called *Mind Your Language*, which represented Indians and Pakistanis as ludicrous caricatures.

Everyone, except the mass of the population, had videos. And I could see why, since Pakistan TV was so peculiar. On my first day I turned it on and a cricket match was taking place. I settled in my chair. But the English players, who were on tour in Pakistan, were leaving the pitch. In fact, Bob Willis and Ian Botham were running towards the dressing rooms surrounded by armed police and this wasn't because Botham had made derogatory remarks about Pakistan. (He said it was a country to which he'd like to send his mother-in-law.) In the background a section of the crowd was being tear-gassed. Then the screen went blank.

Stranger still, and more significant, was the fact that the news was now being read in Arabic, a language few people in Pakistan understood. Someone explained to me that this was because the Koran was in Arabic, but everyone else said it was because

General Zia wanted to kiss the arses of the Arabs.

The man at the party, who was drunk, wanted to tell me something and kept pulling at me. The man was worried. But wasn't I worried too? I was trapped with this woman and the marriage proposal.

I was having a little identity crisis. I'd been greeted so warmly in Pakistan, I felt so excited by what I saw, and so at home with all my uncles, I wondered if I were not better off here than there. And when I said, with a little unnoticed irony, that I was an Englishman, people laughed. They fell about. Why would anyone with a brown face, Muslim name and large well-known family in Pakistan want to lay claim to that cold little decrepit island off Europe where you always had to spell your name? Strangely, anti-British remarks made me feel patriotic, though I only felt patriotic when I was away from England.

But I couldn't allow myself to feel too Pakistani. I didn't want to give in to that falsity, that sentimentality. As someone said to me at a party, provoked by the fact I was wearing jeans: we are Pakistanis, but you, you will always be a Paki – emphasizing the slang derogatory name the English used against Pakistanis, and therefore the fact that I couldn't rightfully lay claim to either place.

In England I was a playwright. In Karachi this meant little. There were no theatres; the arts were discouraged by the state – music and dancing are un-Islamic – and ignored by practically everyone else. So despite everything I felt pretty out of place.

The automatic status I gained through my family obtained for me such acceptance, respect and luxury that for the first time I could understand the privileged and their penchant for marshalling ridiculous arguments to justify their delicious and untenable position as an élite. But as I wasn't a doctor, or businessman or military person, people suspected that this writing business I talked about was a complicated excuse for idleness, uselessness and general bumming around. In fact, as I proclaimed an interest in the entertainment business, and talked much and loudly about how integral the arts were to a society, moves were being made to set me up in the amusement arcade business, in Shepherd's Bush.

Finally the man got me on my own. His name was Rahman. He was a friend of my intellectual uncle. I had many uncles, but Rahman preferred the intellectual one who understood Rahman's particular sorrow and like him considered himself to be a marginal man.

In his fifties, a former Air Force officer, Rahman was liberal, well-travelled and married to an Englishwoman who now had a Pakistani accent.

He said to me: 'I tell you, this country is being sodomized by religion. It is even beginning to interfere with the making of money. And now we are embarked on this dynamic regression, you must know, it is obvious, Pakistan has become a leading country to go away from. Our patriots are abroad. We despise and envy them. For the rest of us, our class, your family, we are in Hobbes's state of nature: insecure, frightened. We cling together out of necessity.' He became optimistic. 'We could be like Japan, a tragic oriental country that is now progressive, industrialized.' He laughed and then said, ambiguously: 'But only God keeps this country together. You must say this around the world: we are taking a great leap backwards.'

The bitterest blow for Rahman was the dancing. He liked to waltz and foxtrot. But now the expression of physical joy, of sensuality and rhythm, was banned. On TV you could see where it had been censored. When couples in Western programmes got up to dance there'd be a jerk in the film, and they'd be sitting down again. For Rahman it was inexplicable, an unnecessary cruelty that was almost more arbitrary than anything else.

Thus the despair of Rahman and my uncles' 'high and dry' generation. Mostly educated in Britain, like Jinnah, the founder of Pakistan – who was a smoking, drinking, non-Urdu speaking lawyer and claimed that Pakistan would never be a theocracy ('that Britisher' he was sometimes called) – their intellectual mentors were Tawney, Shaw, Russell, Laski. For them the new Islamization was the negation of their lives.

It was a lament I heard often. This was the story they told. Karachi was a goodish place in the 1960s and 1970s. Until about 1977 it was lively and vigorous. You could drink and dance in the Raj-style clubs (providing you were admitted) and the atmosphere was liberal – as long as you didn't meddle in politics, in which case you'd probably be imprisoned. Politically there was Bhutto: urbane, Oxford-educated, considering himself to be a poet and revolutionary, a veritable Chairman Mao of the sub-continent. He said he would fight obscurantism and illiteracy, ensure the equality of men and women, and increase access to education and medical care. The desert would bloom.

Later, in an attempt to save himself, appease the mullahs and rouse the dissatisfied masses behind him, he introduced various Koranic injunctions into the constitution and banned alcohol, gambling, horse-racing. The Islamization had begun, and was fervently continued after his execution.

Islamization built no hospitals, no schools, no houses; it cleaned no water and installed no electricity. But it was direction, identity. The country was to be in the hands of the divine, or rather, in the hands of those who elected themselves to interpret the single divine purpose. Under the tyranny of the priesthood, with the cooperation of the army, Pakistan would embody Islam in itself.

There would now be no distinction between ethical and religious obligation; there would now be no areas in which it was possible to be wrong. The only possible incertitude was of interpretation. The theory would be the written eternal and universal principles which Allah created and made obligatory for men; the model would be the first three generations of Muslims; and the practice would be Pakistan.

As a Professor of Law at the Islamic University wrote: 'Pakistan accepts Islam as the basis of economic and political life. We do not have a single reason to make any separation between Islam and Pakistan society. Pakistanis now adhere rigorously to Islam and cling steadfastly to their religious heritage. They never speak of these things with disrespect. With an acceleration in the process of Islamization, governmental capabilities increase and national identity and loyalty become stronger. Because Islamic civilization has brought Pakistanis very close to certainty, this society is ideally imbued with a moral mission.'

This moral mission and the over-emphasis on dogma and punishment, resulted in the kind of strengthening of the repressive, militaristic and nationalistically aggressive state seen all over the world in the authoritarian 1980s. With the added bonus that in Pakistan, God was always on the side of the government.

But despite all the strident nationalism, as Rahman said, the patriots were abroad; people were going away: to the West, to Saudi Arabia, anywhere. Young people continually asked me about the possibility of getting into Britain and some thought of taking some smack with them to bankroll their establishment. They had what was called the Gulf Syndrome, a condition I recognized from my time living in the suburbs. It was a dangerous psychological cocktail consisting of ambition, suppressed excitement, bitterness and sexual longing.

Then a disturbing incident occurred which seemed to encapsulate the going-away fever. An eighteen-year-old girl from a village called Chakwal dreamed that the villagers walked across the Arabian Sea to Karbala where they found money and work. Following this dream the village set off one night for the beach which happened to be near my uncle's house, in fashionable Clifton. Here lived politicians and diplomats in LA-style white bungalows with sprinklers on the lawn, a Mercedes in the drive and dogs and watchmen at the gates.

Here Benazir Bhutto was under house arrest. Her dead father's mansion was patrolled by the army who boredly nursed machine-guns and sat in tents beneath the high walls.

On the beach, the site of barbecues and late-night parties, the men of the Chakwal village packed the women and children into trunks and pushed them into the Arabian Sea. Then they followed them into the water, in the direction of Karbala. All but twenty of the potential *émigrés* were drowned. The survivors were arrested and charged with illegal emigration.

It was the talk of Karachi. It caused much amusement but people like Rahman despaired of a society that could be so confused, so advanced in some respects, so very naïve in others.

And all the (more orthodox) going away disturbed and confused the family set-up. When the men who'd been away came back, they were different, they were dissatisfied, they had seen more, they wanted more. Their neighbours were envious and resentful. Once more the society was being changed by outside forces, not by its own volition.

About twelve people lived permanently in my uncle's house, plus servants who slept in sheds at the back, just behind the chickens and dogs. Relatives sometimes came to stay for months. New bits had to be built on to the house. All day there were visitors; in the evenings crowds of people came over; they were welcome, and they ate and watched videos and talked for hours. People weren't so protective of their privacy as they were in London.

This made me think about the close-bonding within the families and about the intimacy and interference of an extended family and a more public way of life. Was the extended family worse than the little nuclear family because there were more people to dislike? Or better because relationships were less intense?

Strangely, bourgeois-bohemian life in London, in Notting Hill and Islington and Fulham, was far more formal. It was frozen dinner parties and the division of social life into the meeting of couples with other couples, to discuss the lives of other coupling couples. Months would pass, then this would happen again.

In Pakistan, there was the continuity of the various families' knowledge of each other. People were easy to place; your grandparents and theirs were friends. When I went to the bank and showed the teller my passport, it turned out he knew several of my uncles, so I didn't receive the usual perfunctory treatment. This was how things worked.

I compared the collective hierarchy of the family and the permanence of my family's circle, with my feckless, rather rootless life in London, in what was called 'the inner city'. There I lived alone, and lacked any long connection with anything. I'd hardly known anyone for more than eight years, and certainly not their parents. People came and went. There was much false intimacy and forced friendship. People didn't take responsibility for each other.

Many of my friends lived alone in London, especially the women. They wanted to be independent and to enter into relationships – as many as they liked, with whom they liked – out of choice. They didn't merely want to reproduce the old patterns of living. The future was to be determined by choice and reason, not by custom. The notions of duty and obligation barely had positive meaning for my friends; they were loaded, Victorian words, redolent of constraint and grandfather clocks, the antithesis of generosity in love, the new hugging, and the transcendence of the family. The ideal of the new relationship was no longer the S and M of the old marriage – it was F and C, freedom plus commitment.

In the large, old families where there was nothing but the old patterns, disturbed only occasionally by the new ways, this would have seemed a contrivance, a sort of immaturity, a failure to understand and accept the determinacies that life necessarily involved.

So there was much pressure to conform, especially on the women.

'Let these women be warned,' said a mullah to the dissenting women of Rawalpindi. 'We will tear them to pieces. We will give them such terrible punishments that no one in future will dare to raise a voice against Islam.'

I remember a woman saying to me at dinner one night: 'We know at least one thing. God will never dare to show his face in this country – the women will tear him apart!'

The family scrutiny and criticism was difficult to take, as was all the bitching and gossip. But there was warmth and continuity for a large number of people; there was security and much love. Also there was a sense of duty and community – of people's lives genuinely being lived together, whether they liked each other or not – that you didn't get in London. There, those who'd eschewed the family hadn't succeeded in creating some other form of supportive common life. In Pakistan there was that supportive common life, but at the expense of movement and change.

In the 1960s of Enoch Powell and graffiti, the Black Muslims and Malcolm X gave needed strength to the descendants of slaves by 'taking the wraps off the white man'; Eldridge Cleaver was yet to be converted to Christianity and Huey P. Newton was toting his Army .45. A boy in a bedroom in a suburb, who had the King's Road constantly on his mind and who changed the pictures on his wall from week to week, was unhappy, and separated from the 1960s as by a thick glass wall against which he could only press his face. But bits of the 1960s were still around in Pakistan: the liberation rhetoric, for example, the music, the clothes, the drugs, not as the way of life they were originally intended to be, but as appendages to another, stronger tradition.

As my friends and I went into the Bara Market near Peshawar, close to the border of Afghanistan, in a rattling motorized rickshaw, I became apprehensive. There were large signs by the road telling foreigners that the police couldn't take responsibility for them: beyond this point the police would not go. Apparently the Pathans there, who were mostly refugees from Afghanistan, liked to kidnap foreigners and extort ransoms. My friends, who were keen to buy opium, which they'd give to the rickshaw driver to carry, told me everything was all right, because I wasn't a foreigner. I kept forgetting that.

The men were tough, martial, insular and proud. They lived in mud houses and tin shacks built like forts for shooting from. They were inevitably armed, with machine-guns slung over their shoulders. In the street you wouldn't believe women existed here, except you knew they took care of the legions of young men in the area who'd fled from Afghanistan to avoid being conscripted by the Russians and sent to Moscow for re-education.

Ankle deep in mud, I went round the market. Pistols, knives, Russian-made rifles, hand grenades and large lumps of dope and opium were laid out on stalls like tomatoes and oranges. Everyone was selling heroin.

The Americans, who had much money invested in Pakistan, in this compliant right-wing buffer-zone between Afghanistan and India, were furious that their children were being destroyed by a flourishing illegal industry in a country they financed. But the Americans sent to Pakistan could do little about it. Involvement in the heroin trade went right through Pakistan society: the police, the judiciary, the army, the landlords, the customs officials were all involved. After all, there was nothing in the Koran about heroin, nothing specific. I was even told that its export made ideological sense. Heroin was anti-Western; addiction in Western children was a deserved symptom of the moral vertigo of godless societies. It was a kind of colonial revenge. Reverse imperialism, the Karachi wits called it, inviting nemesis. The reverse imperialism was itself being reversed.

In a flat high above Karachi, an eighteen-year-old kid strung-out on heroin danced cheerfully around the room in front of me and pointed to an erection in the front of his trousers, which he referred to as his Imran Khan, the name of the handsome Pakistan cricket captain. More and more of the so-called multinational kids were taking heroin now. My friends who owned the flat, journalists on a weekly paper, were embarrassed.

But they always had dope to offer their friends. These laid-back people were mostly professionals: lawyers, an inspector in the police who smoked what he confiscated, a newspaper magnate, and various other journalists. Heaven it was to smoke at midnight on the beach, as local fishermen, squatting respectfully behind you, fixed fat joints; and the 'erotic politicians' themselves, the Doors, played from a portable stereo while the Arabian Sea rolled on to the beach. Oddly, since heroin and dope were both indigenous to the country, it took the West to make them popular in the East.

In so far as colonizers and colonized engage in a relationship with the latter aspiring to be like the former, you wouldn't catch anyone of my uncle's generation with a joint in their mouth. It was *infra dig* – for the peasants. Shadowing the British, they drank whisky and read *The Times*; they praised others by calling them 'gentlemen'; and their eyes filled with tears at old Vera Lynn records.

But the kids discussed yoga exercises. You'd catch them standing on their heads. They even meditated. Though one boy who worked at the airport said it was too much of a Hindu thing for Muslims to be doing; if his parents caught him chanting a mantra he'd get a backhander across the face. Mostly the kids listened to the Stones, Van Morrison and Bowie as they flew over ruined roads to the beach in bright red and yellow Japanese cars with quadrophonic speakers, past camels and acres of wasteland.

Here, all along the railway track, the poor and diseased and hungry lived in shacks and huts; the filthy poor gathered around rusty stand-pipes to fetch water; or ingeniously they resurrected wrecked cars, usually Morris Minors; and here they slept in huge sewer pipes among buffalo, chickens and wild dogs. Here I met a policeman who I thought was on duty. But the policeman lived here, and hanging on the wall of his falling-down shed was his spare white police uniform, which he'd had to buy himself.

If not to the beach, the kids went to the Happy Hamburger to hang out. Or to each other's houses to watch Clint Eastwood tapes and giggle about sex, of which they were so ignorant and deprived. I watched a group of agitated young men in their mid-twenties gather around a 1950s' medical book to look at the female genitalia. For these boys, who watched Western films and mouthed the lyrics of pop songs celebrating desire ('come on, baby, light my fire'), life before marriage could only be like spending years and years in a single-sex public school; for them women were mysterious, unknown, desirable and yet threatening creatures of almost another species, whom you had to respect, marry and impregnate but couldn't be friends with. And in this country where the sexes were usually strictly segregated, the sexual tension could be palpable. The men who could afford to, flew to Bangkok for relief. The others squirmed and resented women. The kind of sexual openness that was one of the few real achievements of the 1960s, the discussion of contraception, abortion, female sexuality and prostitution which some women were trying to advance received incredible hostility. But women felt it was only a matter of time before progress was made; it was much harder to return to ignorance than the mullahs thought.

A stout intense lawyer in his early thirties of immense extrovert charm – with him it was definitely the 1980s, not the 1960s. His father was a judge. He himself was intelligent, articulate and fiercely representative of the other 'new spirit' of Pakistan. He didn't drink, smoke or fuck. Out of choice. He prayed five times a day. He worked all the time. He was determined to be a good Muslim, since that was the whole point of the country existing at all. He wasn't indulgent, except religiously, and he lived in accordance with what he believed. I took to him immediately.

We had dinner in an expensive restaurant. It could have been in London or New York. The food was excellent, I said. The lawyer disagreed, with his mouth full, shaking his great head. It was definitely no good, it was definitely meretricious rubbish. But for ideological reasons only, I concluded, since he ate with relish. He was only in the restaurant because of me, he said.

There was better food in the villages; the new food in Pakistan was, frankly, a tribute to chemistry rather than cuisine. Only the masses had virtue, they knew how to live, how to eat. He told me that those desiccated others, the marginal men I associated with and liked so much, were a plague class with no values. Perhaps, he suggested, eating massively, this was why I liked them, being English. Their education, their intellectual snobbery, made them un-Islamic. They didn't understand the masses and they spoke in English to cut themselves off from the people. Didn't the best jobs go to those with a foreign education? He was tired of those Westernized elders denigrating their country and its religious nature. They'd been contaminated by the West, they didn't know their own country, and the sooner they got out and were beaten up by racists abroad the better.

The lawyer and I went out into the street. It was busy, the streets full of strolling people. There were dancing camels and a Pakistan trade exhibition. The lawyer strode through it all, yelling. The exhibition was full of Pakistan-made imitations of Western goods: bathrooms in chocolate and strawberry, TVs with stereos attached; fans, air-conditioners, heaters; and an arcade full of space-invaders. The lawyer got agitated.

These were Western things, of no use to the masses. The masses didn't have water, what would they do with strawberry bathrooms? The masses wanted Islam, not space-invaders or . . . or elections. Are elections a Western thing? I asked. Don't they have them in India too? No, they're a Western thing, the lawyer said. How could they be required under Islam? There need only be one party – the party of the righteous.

This energetic lawyer would have pleased and then disappointed Third World intellectuals and revolutionaries from an earlier era, people like Fanon and Guevara. This talk of liberation – at last the acknowledgement of the virtue of the toiling masses, the struggle against neo-colonialism, its bourgeois stooges, and American interference – the entire recognizable rhetoric of freedom and struggle, ends in the lawyer's mind with the country on its knees, at prayer. Having started to look for itself it finds itself . . . in the eighth century.

Islam and the masses. My numerous meetings with scholars, revisionists, liberals who wanted the Koran 'creatively' interpreted to make it compatible with modern science. The many medieval monologues of mullahs I'd listened to. So much talk, theory and Byzantine analysis.

I strode into a room in my uncle's house. Half-hidden by a curtain, on a verandah, was an aged woman servant wearing my cousin's old clothes, praying. I stopped and watched her. In the morning as I lay in bed, she swept the floor of my room with some twigs bound together. She was at least sixty. Now, on the shabby prayer mat, she was tiny and around her the universe was endless, immense, but God was above her. I felt she was acknowledging that which was larger than her, humbling herself before the infinite, knowing and feeling her own insignificance. It was a truthful moment, not empty ritual. I wished I could do it.

I went with the lawyer to the Mosque in Lahore, the largest in the world. I took off my shoes, padded across the immense courtyard with the other man – women were not allowed – and got on my knees. I banged my forehead on the marble floor. Beside me a man in a similar posture gave a world-consuming yawn. I waited but could not lose myself in prayer. I could only travesty the woman's prayer, to whom it had a world of meaning.

Perhaps she did want a society in which her particular moral and religious beliefs were mirrored, and no others, instead of some plural, liberal mélange; a society in which her own cast of mind, her customs, way of life and obedience to God were established with full legal and constituted authority. But it wasn't as if anyone had asked her.

In Pakistan, England just wouldn't go away. Despite the Lahore lawyer, despite everything, England was very much on the minds of Pakistanis. Relics of the Raj were everywhere: buildings, monuments, Oxford accents, libraries full of English books, and newspapers. Many Pakistanis had relatives in England; thousands of Pakistani families depended on money sent from England. Visiting a village, a man told me through an interpreter, that

27

when his three grandchildren visited from Bradford, he had to hire an interpreter to speak to them. It was happening all the time – the closeness of the two societies, and the distance.

Although Pakistanis still wanted to escape to England, the old men in their clubs and the young eating their hamburgers took great pleasure in England's decline and decay. The great master was fallen. Now it was seen as strikebound, drug-ridden, riot-torn, inefficient, disunited, a society which had moved too suddenly from puritanism to hedonism and now loathed itself. And the Karachi wits liked to ask me when I thought the Americans would decide the British were ready for self-government.

Yet people like Rahman still clung to what they called British ideals, maintaining that it is a society's ideals, its conception of human progress, that define the level of its civilization. They regretted, under the Islamization, the repudiation of the values which they said were the only positive aspect of Britain's legacy to the sub-continent. These were: the idea of secular institutions based on reason, not revelation or scripture; the idea that there were no final solutions to human problems; and the idea that the health and vigour of a society was bound up with its ability to tolerate and express a plurality of views on all issues, and that these views would be welcomed.

But England as it is today, the ubiquity of racism and the suffering of Pakistanis because of it, was another, stranger subject. When I talked about it, the response was unexpected. Those who'd been to England often told of being insulted, or beaten up, or harassed at the airport. But even these people had attitudes similar to those who hadn't been there.

It was that the English misunderstood the Pakistanis because they saw only the poor people, those from the villages, the illiterates, the peasants, the Pakistanis who didn't know how to use toilets, how to eat with knives and forks because they were poor. If the British could only see *them*, the rich, the educated, the sophisticated, they wouldn't be so hostile. They'd know what civilized people the Pakistanis really were. And then they'd like them.

The implication was that the poor who'd emigrated to the West to escape the strangulation of the rich in Pakistan, deserved the racism they received in Britain because they really were contemptible. The Pakistani middle class shared the disdain of the British for the *émigré* working class and peasantry of Pakistan.

It was interesting to see that the British working class (and not only the working class, of course) used the same vocabulary of contempt about Pakistanis – the charges of ignorance, laziness, fecklessness, uncleanliness – that their own, British middle class used about them. And they weren't able to see the similarity.

Racism goes hand-in-hand with class inequality. Among other things, racism is a kind of snobbery, a desire to see oneself as superior culturally and economically, and a desire to actively experience and enjoy that superiority by hostility or violence. And when that superiority of class and culture is unsure or not acknowledged by the Other – as it would be acknowledged by the servant and master in class-stable Pakistan – but is in doubt, as with the British working class and Pakistanis in England, then it has to be demonstrated physically. Everyone knows where they stand then – the class inequality is displayed, just as any other snob demonstrates superiority by exhibiting wealth or learning or ancestry.

So some of the middle class of Pakistan, who also used the familiar vocabulary of contempt about their own poor (and, incidentally, about the British poor) couldn't understand when I explained that British racists weren't discriminating in their racial discrimination: they loathed all Pakistanis and kicked whoever was nearest. To the English all Pakistanis were the same; racists didn't ask whether you had a chauffeur, TV and private education before they set fire to your house. But for some Pakistanis, it was their own poor who had brought this upon them.

Three: England

It has been an arduous journey. Since Enoch Powell in the 1960s, there have been racist marches through South London approved by the Labour Home Secretary; attacks by busloads of racists on Southall, which the Asians violently and successfully repelled;

and the complicated affair of young Asians burned to death and Asian shops razed to the ground by young blacks in Handsworth, Birmingham. The insults, the beatings, the murders continue. Although there has been white anger and various race relations legislation, Pakistanis are discriminated against in all areas.

Powell's awful prophecy was fulfilled: the hate he worked to create and the party of which he was a member, brought about his prediction. The River Tiber has indeed over-flowed with much blood – Pakistani blood. And seventeen years later Powell has once more called for repatriation, giving succour to those who hate.

The fight back is under way. The defence committees, vigilante groups, study groups, trade union and women's groups are flourishing. People have changed, become united, through struggle and self-defence. My white friends, like Bog Brush, didn't enjoy fighting Pakistanis. They had a reputation for premature sobbing and cowardice. You didn't get your money's worth fighting a Paki. That's quite different now.

The fierce truculent pride of the Black Panthers is here now, as is the separatism, the violence, the bitterness and pathetic elevation of an imaginary homeland. This is directly spawned by racism.

Our cities are full of Asian shops. Where one would want black united with black, there are class differences as with all groups. Those Pakistanis who have worked hard to establish businesses, now vote Tory and give money to the Conservative Party. Their interests are the same as those of middle-class business people everywhere, though they are subject to more jealousy and violence. They have wanted to elevate themselves out of the maelstrom and by gaining economic power and the opportunity and dignity it brings, they have made themselves safe – safer. They have taken advantage of England.

But what is the Conservative view of them? Roger Scruton in his book *The Meaning Of Conservatism* sets out the case against mutual respect and understanding.

Firstly he deplores all race relations legislation and tries to justify certain kinds of racism by making it seem a harmless preference for certain kinds of people. He calls this preference a 'natural offshoot' of allegiance. Secondly, and more tellingly he says that 'illiberal sentiments . . . arise inevitably from social consciousness: they involve natural prejudice, and a desire for the company of one's kind. That is hardly sufficient ground to condemn them as "racist".'

The crucial Conservative idea here is Scruton's notion of 'the company of one's kind'. What is the company of one's kind? Who exactly is of one's kind and what kind of people are they? Are they only those of the same 'nation', of the same colour, race and background? I suspect that that is what Scruton intends. But what a feeble, bloodless, narrow conception of human relationships and the possibilities of love and communication that he can only see 'one's kind' in this exclusive and complacent way!

One does seek the company of one's kind, of those in the same street, in the same club, in the same office. But the idea that these are the only people one can get along with or identify with, that one's humanity is such a heldback thing that it can't extend beyond this, leads to the denigration of those unlike oneself. It leads to the idea that others have less humanity than oneself or one's own group or 'kind'; and to the idea of the Enemy, of the alien, of the Other. As Baldwin says: 'this inevitably leads to murder', and of course it has often done so in England recently.

Scruton quotes approvingly those who call this view 'death camp chic'. He would argue, I suppose, that loyalty and allegiance to one's kind doesn't necessarily lead to loathing of those not of one's kind. But Scruton himself talks of the 'alien wedge' and says that 'immigration cannot be an object of merely passive contemplation on the part of the present citizenship'.

The evil of racism is that it is a violation not only of another's dignity, but also of one's own person or soul; the failure of connection with others is a failure to understand or feel what it is one's own humanity consists in, what it is to be alive, and what it is to see both oneself and others as being ends not means, and as having souls. However much anodyne talk there is of 'one's kind', a society that is racist is a society that cannot accept itself, that hates parts of itself so deeply that it cannot see, does not want to see – because of its spiritual and political nullity and inanition – how much people have in common with each other. And the whole society and every element in it, is reduced and degraded

31

because of it. This is why racism isn't a minor or sub-problem: it reflects on the whole and weighs the entire society in the balance.

Therefore, in the end, one's feeling for others, one's under-standing of their humanity cannot be anything to do with their being of 'one's kind' in the narrow way Scruton specifies. It can't be to do with others having any personal qualities at all. For paradoxically, as Simone Weil says: 'So far from its being his person, what is sacred in a human being is the impersonal in him. Everything which is impersonal in man is sacred, and nothing else.'

What of Labour?

The Pakistani working class is as unprotected politically as it has ever been. Despite various paternalistic efforts and an attempt at a kind of 'Raj decency', racism is the Trojan Horse within the labour movement. The Labour Party has failed to show that it is serious about combating racism and serious in representing the black working class. There are few black councillors, few black parliamentary candidates, few blacks on the General Management Committees of constituency Labour Parties, no blacks on the NEC and so on, right through the Labour and trade union movement.

In my own ward and management committee, I have seen racist attitudes that would shame some Tories. People have stood up at Labour Party meetings I have attended and delivered racist diatribes. I have seen blacks discouraged from joining the Labour Party, and when they have joined, actively discouraged from canvassing in case they discouraged white racists from voting Labour.

The Labour Party wishes to be egalitarian and liberal on the race issue but knows that vast numbers of its voters are neither. The party is afraid – in some parts consciously and in other parts unconsciously – that blacks and black issues are a vote loser. If the Labour Party occasionally wishes blacks to serve it, it does not desire to serve blacks. Hence it acknowledges that thousands of its supporters are racist. It refuses to confront that.

Others in the party believe that racism is a sub-issue which has to be subordinate to the class issues of the time: housing, unemployment, education, maintenance of the social services and so on. They believe that winning elections and representing the mass of the working class in Parliament is more important than giving office or power to blacks. This is the choice it has made. This is the kind of party it is, and insofar as this is true, the Labour Party is a truly representative party, representing inequality and racism.

Coming back to England was harder than going. I had culture shock in reverse. Images of plenty yelled at me. England seemed to be overflowing with . . . things. Things from all over the world. Things and information. Information though, which couldn't bite through the profound insularity and indifference.

In Pakistan people were keen to know: not only about Asia and the Middle East, but about Europe and the United States. They sought out information about the whole world. They needed it. They ordered books from Europe, listened to international radio and chewed up visiting academics like pieces of orange.

In Britain today, among the middle class, thinking and argument are almost entirely taboo. The other taboo, replacing death in its unacceptability, is money. As our society has become more divided, the acknowledgement of that division – which is a financial division, a matter of economic power – is out of the question. So money is not discussed. It is taken for granted that you have it: that you have means of obtaining it: that you are reasonably well off and gain status and influence over others because of it.

Accompanying this financial silence, and shoring up both the social division and the taboo, is the prohibition on thought. The discussion of a serious subject to a conclusion using logic, evidence and counter-evidence is an unacceptable social embarrassment. It just isn't done to argue: it is thought to be the same as rowing. One has opinions in England, but they are formed in private and clung to in public despite everything, despite their often being quite wrong.

There is real defensiveness and insecurity, a Victorian fear of revealing so much as a genital of an idea, the nipple of a notion or the sex of a syllogism. Where sexual exhibitionism and the discussion of positions and emissions is fashionable, indeed orthodox, thinking and argument are avoided.

In Pakistan it was essential to have knowledge because political discussion was serious. It mattered what you thought. People put chairs in a circle, sat down, and *talked*. What was said to each other was necessary. Intellectual dignity was maintained, earned anxiety was expressed; you weren't alone; ideas and feelings were shared. These things had to be said, even in low voices, because absolute silence was intolerable, absolute silence was the acceptance of isolation and division. It was a relief to argue, to exercise intelligence in a country where intelligence was in itself a weapon and a threat.

I will never forget the hospitality, warmth and generosity of the people of Pakistan; the flowers on the lawn of the Sind Club, the sprawling open houses, full of air and people and the smell of spices; the unbelievable brightness of the light shining through a dust haze; the woman walking perfectly straight-backed along a street with an iron balanced on her head; the open-air typists outside the law courts; butterflies as big as clock faces; the man who slept with a chicken in his bed; my uncle's library, bought in the 1940s in Cambridge, where he was taught by Russell – though when I opened the books after being given the library, they were rotten with worms, the pitted pages falling apart just as I stood there. And the way the men shake hands. This is worth going into.

First you offer them your hand and they grasp it. The clasped hands are slapped then with their spare hand as an affirmation of initial contact. This is, as it were, the soup. Now they pull you to them for the main course, the full embrace, the steak. As you look over their shoulder, your bodies thrust together, your heat intermingled, they crack you on the back at least three times with their open palm. These are not negligible taps, but good healthy whacks, demonstrating equality and openness. Depending on the nature of the friendship, these whacks could go on a considerable time and may debilitate the sick or weak. But they must be reciprocated. This done, they will let you move away from them, but still holding your right hand. You are considered fully, with affection overbrimming, as they regard all of you, as they seem to take in your entire being from top to toe, from inside to out. At last, after complete contact has been made, all possibility of concealment or inhibition banished, they carefully let go of your hand as if it were a delicate object. *That is a greeting*.

And there was the photograph of my father in my uncle's room, in which he must have been about the same age as me. A picture in a house that contained fragments of my past: a house full of stories, of Bombay, Delhi, China; of feuds, wrestling matches, adulteries, windows broken with hands, card games, impossible loves, and magic spells. Stories to help me see my place in the world and give me a sense of the past which could go into making a life in the present and the future. This was surely part of the way I could understand myself. This knowledge, garnered in my mid-twenties, would help me form an image of myself: I'd take it back to England where I needed it to protect myself. And it would be with me in London and the suburbs, making me stronger.

When I considered staying in Pakistan to regain more of my past and complete myself with it, I had to think that that was impossible. Didn't I already miss too much of England? And wasn't I too impatient with the illiberalism and lack of possibility of Pakistan?

So there was always going to be the necessary return to England. I came home . . . to my country.

This is difficult to say. 'My country' isn't a notion that comes easily. It is still difficult to answer the question, where do you come from? I have never wanted to identify with England. When Enoch Powell spoke for England I turned away in final disgust. I would rather walk naked down the street than stand up for the National Anthem. The pain of that period of my life, in the mid-1960s, is with me still. And when I originally wrote this piece I put it in the third person: Hanif saw this, Hanif felt that, because of the difficulty of directly addressing myself to what I felt then, of not wanting to think about it again. And perhaps that is why I took to writing in the first place, to make strong feelings into weak feelings.

But despite all this, some kind of identification with England remains.

It is strange to go away to the land of your ancestors, to find out how much you have in common with people there, yet at the same time to realize how British you are, the extent to which, as Orwell

35

says: 'the suet puddings and the red pillar boxes have entered into your soul'. It isn't *that* you wanted to find out. But it is part of what you do find out. And you find out what little choice you have in the matter of your background and where you belong. You look forward to getting back; you think often of England and what it means to you – and you think often of what it means to be British.

Two days after my return I took my washing to a laundrette and gave it to the attendant only to be told she didn't touch the clothes of foreigners: she didn't want me anywhere near her blasted laundrette. More seriously: I read in the paper that a Pakistani family in the East End had been fire-bombed. A child was killed. This, of course, happens frequently. It is the pig's head through the window, the spit in the face, the children with the initials of racist organizations tattooed into their skin with razor blades, as well as the more polite forms of hatred.

I was in a rage. I thought: who wants to be British anyway? Or as a black American writer said: who wants to be integrated into a burning house anyway?

And indeed I know Pakistanis and Indians born and brought up here who consider their position to be the result of a diaspora: they are in exile, awaiting return to a better place, where they belong, where they are welcome. And there this 'belonging' will be total. This will be home, and peace.

It is not difficult to see how much illusion and falsity there is in this view. How much disappointment and unhappiness might be involved in going 'home' only to see the extent to which you have been formed by England and the depth of attachment you feel to the place, despite everything.

It isn't surprising that some people believe in this idea of 'home'. The alternative to believing it is more conflict here; it is more self-hatred; it is the continual struggle against racism; it is the continual adjustment to life in Britain. And blacks in Britain know they have made more than enough adjustments.

So what is it to be British?

In his 1941 essay 'England Your England' Orwell says: 'the gentleness of the English civilisation is perhaps its most marked characteristic'. He calls the country 'a family with the wrong members in control' and talks of the 'soundness and homogeneity of England'.

Elsewhere he considers the Indian character. He explains the 'maniacal suspiciousness' which, agreeing, he claims, with E. M. Forster in *A Passage To India*, he calls 'the besetting Indian vice . . .' But he has the grace to acknowledge in his essay 'Not Counting Niggers' 'that the overwhelming bulk of the British proletariat [lives] . . . in Asia and Africa'.

But this is niggardly. The main object of his praise is British 'tolerance' and he writes of 'their gentle manners'. He also says that this aspect of England 'is continuous, it stretches into the future and the past, there is something in it that persists'.

But does it persist? If this version of England was true then, in the 1930s and 1940s, it is under pressure now. From the point of view of thousands of black people it just does not apply. It is completely without basis.

Obviously tolerance in a stable, confident wartime society with a massive Empire is quite different to tolerance in a disintegrating uncertain society during an economic depression. But surely this would be the test; this would be just the time for this much-advertised tolerance in the British soul to manifest itself as more than vanity and self-congratulation. But it has not. Under real continuous strain it has failed.

Tolerant, gentle British whites have no idea how little of this tolerance is experienced by blacks here. No idea of the violence, hostility and contempt directed against black people every day by state and individual alike in this land once described by Orwell as being not one of 'rubber truncheons' or 'Jew-baiters' but of 'flower-lovers' with 'mild knobbly faces'. But in parts of England the flower-lovers are all gone, the rubber truncheons and Jew-baiters are at large, and if any real contemporary content is to be given to Orwell's blind social patriotism, then clichés about 'tolerance' must be seriously examined for depth and weight of substantial content.

In the meantime it must be made clear that blacks don't require 'tolerance' in this particular condescending way. It isn't this particular paternal tyranny that is wanted, since it is major adjustments to British society that have to be made.

37

I stress that it is the British who have to make these adjustments.

It is the British, the white British, who have to learn that being British isn't what it was. Now it is a more complex thing, involving new elements. So there must be a fresh way of seeing Britain and the choices it faces: and a new way of being British after all this time. Much thought, discussion and self-examination must go into seeing the necessity for this, what this 'new way of being British' involves and how difficult it might be to attain.

The failure to grasp this opportunity for a revitalized and broader self-definition in the face of a real failure to be human, will be more insularity, schism, bitterness and catastrophe.

The two countries, Britain and Pakistan, have been part of each other for years, usually to the advantage of Britain. They cannot now be wrenched apart, even if that were desirable. Their futures will be intermixed. What that intermix means, its moral quality, whether it is violently resisted by ignorant whites and character-ized by inequality and injustice, or understood, accepted and humanized, is for all of us to decide.

This decision is not one about a small group of irrelevant people who can be contemptuously described as 'minorities'. It is about the direction of British society. About its values and how humane it can be when experiencing real difficulty and possible breakdown. It is about the respect it accords individuals, the power it gives to groups, and what it really means when it describes itself as 'democratic'. The future is in our hands.

Introduction to *My Beautiful Laundrette*

I wrote the script of *My Beautiful Laundrette* in my uncle's house in Karachi, Pakistan, in February 1985, during the night. As I wrote, cocks crowed and the call to prayer reverberated through crackly speakers from a nearby mosque. It was impossible to sleep. One morning as I sat on the verandah having breakfast, I had a phone call from Howard Davies, a director with the Royal Shakespeare Company, with whom I'd worked twice before. He wanted to direct Brecht's *Mother Courage*, with Judi Dench in the lead role. He wanted me to adapt it.

That summer, back in England and at Howard's place in Stratford-upon-Avon, I sat in the orchard with two pads of paper in front of me: on one I rewrote *My Beautiful Laundrette* and on the other I adapted Brecht from a literal translation into language that could be spoken by the RSC actors.

As *Laundrette* was the first film I'd written, and I was primarily a playwright, I wrote each scene of the film like a little scene for a play, with the action written like stage directions and with lots of dialogue. Then I'd cut most of the dialogue and add more stage directions, often set in cars, or with people running about, to keep the thing moving, since films required action.

I'd had a couple of lunches with Karin Banborough of Channel Four. She wanted me to write something for *Film on Four*. I was extremely keen. For me *Film on Four* had taken over from the BBC's *Play For Today* in presenting serious contemporary drama on TV to a wide audience. The work of TV writers like Alan Bennett (much of it directed by Stephen Frears), Dennis Potter, Harold Pinter, Alan Plater and David Mercer, influenced me greatly when I was young and living at home in the suburbs. On my way up to London the morning after a *Play For Today* I'd sit in the train listening to people discussing the previous night's drama and interrupt them with my own opinions.

The great advantage of TV drama was that people watched it; difficult, challenging things could be said about contemporary life. The theatre, despite the efforts of touring companies and so on, has failed to get its ideas beyond a small enthusiastic audience.

When I finished a draft of *My Beautiful Laundrette*, and *Mother Courage* had gone into rehearsal, Karin Banborough, David Rose and I discussed directors for the film.

A couple of days later I went to see a friend, David Gothard, who was then running Riverside Studios. I often went for a walk by the river in the early evening, and then I'd sit in David's office. He always had the new books and the latest magazines; and whoever was appearing at Riverside would be around. Riverside stood for tolerance, scepticism and intelligence. The feeling there was that works of art, plays, books and so on, were important. This is a rare thing in England. For many writers, actors, dancers and artists, Riverside was what a university should be: a place to learn and talk and work and meet your contemporaries. There was no other place like it in London and David Gothard was the great encourager, getting work on and introducing people to one another.

He suggested I ask Stephen Frears to direct the film. I thought this an excellent idea, except that I admired Frears too much to have the nerve to ring him. David Gothard did this and I cycled to Stephen's house in Notting Hill, where he lived in a street known as 'director's row' because of the number of film directors living there.

He said he wanted to shoot my film in February. As it was November already I pointed out that February might be a little soon. Would there be time to prepare, to rewrite? But he had a theory: when you have a problem, he said, bring things forward; do them sooner rather than later. And anyway, February was a good month for him; he made his best films then; England looked especially unpleasant; and people worked faster in the cold.

The producers, Tim Bevan and Sarah Radclyffe, Stephen had worked with before, on promos for rock bands. So the film was set up and I started to rewrite. Stephen and I had long talks, each of us pacing up and down the same piece of carpet, in different directions.

The film started off as an epic. It was to be like *The Godfather*, opening in the past with the arrival of an immigrant family in England and showing their progress to the present. There were to be many scenes set in the 1950s; people would eat bread and dripping and get off boats a lot; there would be scenes of Johnny and Omar as children and large-scale set pieces of racist marches with scenes of mass violence.

We soon decided it was impossible to make a film of such scale. That film is still to be made. Instead I set the film in the present, though references to the past remain.

It was shot in six weeks in February and March of 1985 on a low budget and 16mm film. For this I was glad. There were no commercial pressures on us, no one had a lot of money invested in the film who could tell us what to do. And I was tired of seeing lavish films set in exotic locations; it seemed to me that anyone could make such films, providing they had an old book, a hot country, new technology and were capable of aiming the camera at an attractive landscape in the hot country in front of which stood a star in a perfectly clean costume delivering lines from the old book.

We decided the film was to have gangster and thriller elements, since the gangster film is the form that corresponds most closely to the city, with its gangs and violence. And the film was to be an amusement, despite its references to racism, unemployment and Thatcherism. Irony is the modern mode, a way of commenting on bleakness and cruelty without falling into dourness and didacticism. And ever since the first time I heard people in a theatre laugh during a play of mine, I've wanted it to happen again and again.

We found actors – Saeed Jaffrey, for whom I'd written the part; and Roshan Seth I'd seen in David Hare's play *Map Of The World*, commanding that huge stage at the National with complete authority. I skidded through the snow to see Shirley Ann Field and on arriving at her flat was so delighted by her charm and enthusiasm, and so ashamed of the smallness of her part, that there and then I added the material about the magic potions, the moving furniture and the walking trousers. It must have seemed that the rest of the film was quite peripheral and she would be playing the lead in a kind of 'Exorcist' movie with a gay Pakistani, a drug-dealer and a fluff-drying spin-drier in the background.

Soon we stood under railway bridges in Vauxhall at two in the morning in March; we knocked the back wall out of someone's flat and erected a platform outside to serve as the balcony of Papa's flat, which had so many railway lines dipping and criss-crossing beside and above it that inside it you shook like peas in maracas; in an old shop we built a laundrette of such authenticity that people came in off the street with their washing; and I stood on the set making up dialogue before the actors did it themselves, and added one or two new scenes.

When shooting was finished and we had about two-and-a-quarter hours of material strung together, we decided to have a showing for a group of 'wise ones'. They would be film directors, novelists and film writers who'd give us their opinions and thereby aid in editing the film. So I sat at the back of the small viewing cinema as they watched the film. We then cut forty-five minutes out.

The film played at the Edinburgh Film Festival and then went into the cinema.

The script printed here is the last draft before shooting. I haven't attempted to update it or cut out the scenes which were not used in the final version, since it may be of interest to people to compare script with film.

I must thank my friends Walter Donohue, David Gothard, Salman Rushdie, David Nokes and, of course, Sally Whitman, without whom.

My Beautiful Laundrette

My Beautiful Laundrette was first shown at the Edinburgh Film Festival in autumn 1985. The film opened at the London Film Festival on 15 November and was subsequently released at London cinemas on 16 November 1985.

The cast included:

JOHNNY	Daniel Day Lewis
GENGHIS	Richard Graham
SALIM	Derrick Branche
OMAR	Gordon Warnecke
PAPA	Roshan Seth
NASSER	Saeed Jaffrey
RACHEL	Shirley Anne Field
BILQUIS	Charu Bala Choksi
CHERRY	Souad Faress
TANIA	Rita Wolf
ZAKI	Gurdial Sira
MOOSE	Stephen Marcus
GANG MEMBER ONE	Dawn Archibald
GANG MEMBER TWO	Jonathan Moore

Photography   Oliver Stapleton
Film Editor   Mick Audsley
Designer   Hugo Luczyc Wyhowski
Sound Recordist   Albert Bailey
Music   Ludus Tonalis
Casting   Debbie McWilliams
Costume Design   Lindy Hemming
Make-up   Elaine Carew

Screenplay   Hanif Kureishi
Producers   Sarah Radclyffe and Tim Bevan
Director   Stephen Frears

1.   EXT. OUTSIDE A LARGE DETACHED HOUSE. DAY.
CHERRY *and* SALIM *get out of their car. Behind them, the* FOUR
JAMAICANS *get out of their car.*

CHERRY *and* SALIM *walk towards the house. It is a large
falling-down place, in South London. It's quiet at the moment –
early morning – but the ground floor windows are boarded up.*

*On the boarded-up windows is painted: 'Your greed will be the
death of us all' and 'We will defeat the running wogs of capitalism'
and 'Opium is the opium of the unemployed'.*

CHERRY *and* SALIM *look up at the house. The* FOUR
JAMAICANS *stand behind them, at a respectful distance.*

CHERRY: I don't even remember buying this house at the
     auction. What are we going to do with it?

SALIM: Tomorrow we start to renovate it.

CHERRY: How many people are living here?

SALIM: There are no people living here. There are only
     squatters. And they're going to be renovated – right now.
     (*And* SALIM *pushes* CHERRY *forward, giving her the key.*
     CHERRY *goes to the front door of the house.* SALIM, *with* TWO
     JAMAICANS *goes round the side of the house.* TWO
     JAMAICANS *go round the other side.*)

2.   INT. A ROOM IN THE SQUAT. DAY.
GENGHIS *and* JOHNNY *are living in a room in the squat. It is
freezing cold, with broken windows.* GENGHIS *is asleep on a
mattress, wrapped up. He has the flu.* JOHNNY *is lying frozen in a
deck chair, with blankets over him. He has just woken up.*

3.   EXT. OUTSIDE THE HOUSE. DAY.
CHERRY *tries to unlock the front door of the place. But the door has
been barred. She looks in through the letter box. A barricade has
been erected in the hall.*

4. EXT. THE SIDE OF THE HOUSE. DAY.
The JAMAICANS *break into the house through side windows. They
climb in.* SALIM *also climbs into the house.*

5. INT. INSIDE THE HOUSE. DAY.
The JAMAICANS *and* SALIM *are in the house now.*

The JAMAICANS *are kicking open the doors of the squatted rooms.
The* SQUATTERS *are unprepared, asleep or half-awake, in disarray.*

The JAMAICANS *are going from room to room, yelling for everyone
to leave now or get thrown out of the windows with their belongings.*

Some SQUATTERS *complain but they are shoved out of their rooms
into the hall; or down the stairs.* SALIM *is eager about all of this.*

6. INT. GENGHIS AND JOHNNY'S ROOM. DAY.
JOHNNY *looks up the corridor to see what's happening. He goes back
into the room quickly and starts stuffing his things into a black plastic
bag. He is shaking* GENGHIS *at the same time.*
GENGHIS: I'm ill.
JOHNNY: We're moving house.
GENGHIS: No, we've got to fight.
JOHNNY: Too early in the morning.
    (*He rips the blankets off* GENGHIS, *who lies there fully dressed,
    coughing and shivering. A* JAMAICAN *bursts into the room.*)
    All right, all right.
    (*The* JAMAICAN *watches a moment as* GENGHIS, *too weak to
    resist, but cursing violently, takes the clothes* JOHNNY *shoves at
    him and follows* JOHNNY *to the window.* JOHNNY *opens the
    broken window.*)

7. EXT. OUTSIDE THE HOUSE. DAY.
A wide shot of the house.

The SQUATTERS *are leaving through windows and the re-opened
front door and gathering in the front garden, arranging their wretched
belongings. Some of them are junkies. They look dishevelled and
disheartened.*

*From an upper room in the house come crashing a guitar, a TV
and some records. This is followed by the enquiring head of a*
JAMAICAN, *looking to see these have hit no one.*

50

One SQUATTER, *in the front garden, is resisting and a*
JAMAICAN *is holding him. The* SQUATTER *screams at* CHERRY:
you pig, you scum, you filthy rich shit, etc.

As SALIM *goes to join* CHERRY, *she goes to the screaming*
SQUATTER *and gives him a hard backhander across the face.*

8.   EXT. THE BACK OF THE HOUSE. DAY.
JOHNNY *and* GENGHIS *stumble down through the back garden of
the house and over the wall at the end,* JOHNNY *pulling and helping
the exhausted* GENGHIS.

At no time do they see CHERRY *or* SALIM.

9.   INT. BATHROOM. DAY.
OMAR *has been soaking Papa's clothes in the bath. He pulls them
dripping from the bath and puts them in an old steel bucket, wringing
them out. He picks up the bucket.*

10.   EXT. BALCONY. DAY.
OMAR *is hanging out Papa's dripping pyjamas on the washing line
on the balcony, pulling them out of the bucket.*

*The balcony overlooks several busy railway lines, commuter routes
into Charing Cross and London Bridge, from the suburbs.*

OMAR *turns and looks through the glass of the balcony door into
the main room of the flat.* PAPA *is lying in bed. He pours himself
some vodka. Water from the pyjamas drips down Omar's trousers
and into his shoes.*

*When he turns away, a train, huge, close, fast, crashes towards
the camera and bangs and rattles its way past, a few feet from the
exposed overhanging balcony.* OMAR *is unperturbed.*

11.   INT. PAPA'S ROOM. DAY.
The flat OMAR *and his father,* PAPA, *share in South London. It's a
small, damp and dirty place which hasn't been decorated for years.*

PAPA *is as thin as a medieval Christ: an unkempt alcoholic. His
hair is long; his toenails uncut; he is unshaven and scratches his arse
shamelessly. Yet he is not without dignity.*

His bed is in the living room. PAPA *never leaves the bed and
watches TV most of the time.*

51

By the bed is a photograph of Papa's dead wife, Mary. And on the bed is an address book and the telephone.

PAPA *empties the last of a bottle of vodka into a filthy glass. He rolls the empty bottle under the bed.*

OMAR *is now pushing an old-fashioned and ineffective carpet sweeper across the floor.* PAPA *looks at* OMAR's *face. He indicates that* OMAR *should move his face closer, which* OMAR *reluctantly does. To amuse himself,* PAPA *squashes* OMAR's *nose and pulls his cheeks, shaking the boy's unamused face from side to side.*

PAPA: I'm fixing you with a job. With your uncle. Work now, till you go back to college. If your face gets any longer here you'll overbalance. Or I'll commit suicide.

12. INT. KITCHEN. DAY.

OMAR *is in the kitchen of the flat, stirring a big saucepan of dall. He can see through the open door his* FATHER *speaking on the phone to* NASSER. PAPA *speaks in Urdu. 'How are you?' he says. 'And Bilquis? And Tania and the other girls?'*

PAPA: (*Into phone*) Can't you give Omar some work in your garage for a few weeks, yaar? The bugger's your nephew after all.

NASSER: (*VO on phone*) Why do you want to punish me?

13. INT. PAPA'S ROOM. DAY.

PAPA *is speaking to* NASSER *on the phone. He watches* OMAR *slowly stirring dall in the kitchen.* OMAR *is, of course, listening.*

PAPA: He's on dole like everyone else in England. What's he doing home? Just roaming and moaning.

NASSER: (*VO on phone*) Haven't you trained him up to look after you, like I have with my girls?

PAPA: He brushes the dust from one place to another. He squeezes shirts and heats soup. But that hardly stretches him. Though his food stretches me. It's only for a few months, yaar. I'll send him to college in the autumn.

NASSER: (*VO*) He failed once. He had this chronic laziness that runs in our family except for me.

PAPA: If his arse gets lazy – kick it. I'll send a certificate giving permission. And one thing more. Try and fix him with a nice girl. I'm not sure if his penis is in full working order.

14. INT. FLAT. DAY.
Later. OMAR *puts a full bottle of vodka on the table next to Papa's bed.*
PAPA: Go to your uncle's garage.
   (*And* PAPA *pours himself a vodka.* OMAR *quickly thrusts a bottle of tomato juice towards* PAPA, *which* PAPA *ignores. Before* PAPA *can take a swig of the straight vodka,* OMAR *grabs the glass and adds tomato juice.* PAPA *takes it.*)
   If Nasser wants to kick you – let him. I've given permission in two languages. (*To the photograph.*) The bloody's doing me a lot of good. Eh, bloody Mary?

15. EXT. STREET. DAY.
OMAR *walks along a South London street, towards* NASSER's *garage. It's a rough area, beautiful in its own falling-down way.*
   A youngish white BUSKER *is lying stoned in the doorway of a boarded-up shop, his guitar next to him.* OMAR *looks at him.*
   Walking towards OMAR *from an amusement arcade across the street are* JOHNNY *and* GENGHIS *and* MOOSE. GENGHIS *is a well-built white man carrying a pile of right-wing newspapers, badges etc.* MOOSE *is a big white man,* GENGHIS's *lieutenant.*
   JOHNNY *is an attractive man in his early twenties, quick and funny.*
   OMAR *doesn't see* JOHNNY *but* JOHNNY *sees him and is startled. To avoid* OMAR, *in the middle of the road,* JOHNNY *takes* GENGHIS's *arm a moment.*
   GENGHIS *stops suddenly.* MOOSE *charges into the back of him.* GENGHIS *drops the newspapers.* GENGHIS *remonstrates with* MOOSE. JOHNNY *watches* OMAR *go. The traffic stops while* MOOSE *picks up the newspapers.* GENGHIS *starts to sneeze.* MOOSE *gives him a handkerchief.*
   They walk across the road, laughing at the waiting traffic.
   They know the collapsed BUSKER. *He could even be a member of the gang.* JOHNNY *still watches* OMAR's *disappearing back.*
   GENGHIS *and* MOOSE *prepare the newspapers.*
JOHNNY: (*Indicating* OMAR) That kid. We were like that.

GENGHIS: (*Sneezing over* MOOSE's *face*) You don't believe in nothing.

16.   INT. UNDERGROUND GARAGE. DAY.
Uncle Nasser's garage. It's a small private place where wealthy businessmen keep their cars during the day. It's almost full and contains about fifty cars – all Volvos, Rolls-Royces, Mercedes, Rovers, etc.
   At the end of the garage is a small glassed-in office.
   OMAR *is walking down the ramp and into the garage.*

17.   INT. GARAGE OFFICE. DAY.
The glassed-in office contains a desk, a filing cabinet, a typewriter, phone etc. With NASSER *is* SALIM.
   SALIM *is a Pakistani in his late thirties, well-dressed in an expensive, smooth and slightly vulgar way. He moved restlessly about the office. Then he notices* OMAR *wandering about the garage. He watches him.*
   Meanwhile, NASSER *is speaking on the phone in the background.*
NASSER: (*Into phone*) We've got one parking space, yes. It's £25 a week. And from this afternoon we provide a special on the premises 'clean-the-car' service. New thing.
   (*From Salim's POV in the office, through the glass, we see* OMAR *trying the door of one of the cars.* SALIM *goes quickly out of the office.*)

18.   INT. GARAGE. DAY.
SALIM *stands outside the office and shouts at* OMAR. *The sudden sharp voice in the echoing garage.*
SALIM: Hey! Is that your car? Why are you feeling it up then?
   (OMAR *looks at him.*) Come here. Here, I said.

19.   INT. GARAGE OFFICE. DAY.
NASSER *puts down the phone.*

20.   INT. GARAGE OFFICE. DAY.
NASSER *is embracing* OMAR *vigorously, squashing him to him and bashing him lovingly on the back.*

NASSER: (*Introducing him to* SALIM) This one who nearly beat you up is Salim. You'll see a lot of him.

SALIM: (*Shaking hands with* OMAR) I've heard many great things about your father.

NASSER: (*To* OMAR) I must see him. Oh God, how have I got time to do anything?

SALIM: You're too busy keeping this damn country in the black. Someone's got to do it.

NASSER: (*To* OMAR) Your papa, he got thrown out of that clerk's job I fixed him with? He was pissed?

(OMAR *nods.* NASSER *looks regretfully at the boy.*)

Can you wash a car?

(OMAR *looks uncertain.*)

SALIM: Have you washed a car before?

(OMAR *nods.*)

Your uncle can't pay you much. But you'll be able to afford a decent shirt and you'll be with your own people. Not in a dole queue. Mrs Thatcher will be pleased with me.

21.   INT. GARAGE. DAY.

SALIM *and* OMAR *walk across the garage towards a big car.* OMAR *carries a full bucket of water and a cloth. He listens to* SALIM.

SALIM: It's easy to wash a car. You just wet a rag and rub. You know how to rub, don't you?

(*The bucket is overfull.* OMAR *carelessly bangs it against his leg. Water slops out.* SALIM *dances away irritably.* OMAR *walks on.* SALIM *points to a car.* RACHEL *swings down the ramp and into the garage, gloriously.*)

Hi, baby.

RACHEL: My love.

(*And she goes into the garage office. We see her talking and laughing with* NASSER.)

SALIM: (*Indicating car*) And you do this one first. Carefully, as if you were restoring a Renaissance painting. It's my car.

(OMAR *looks up and watches as* RACHEL *and* NASSER *go out through the back of the garage office into the room at the back.*)

22.   INT. ROOM AT BACK OF GARAGE OFFICE. DAY.

RACHEL *and* NASSER, *half-undressed, are drinking, laughing and screwing on a bulging sofa in the wrecked room behind the office, no bigger than a large cupboard.* RACHEL *is bouncing up and down on his huge stomach in her red corset and outrageous worn-for-a-joke underwear.*

NASSER: Rachel, fill my glass, darling.

 (RACHEL *does so, then she begins to move on him.*)

RACHEL: Fill mine.

NASSER: What am I, Rachel, your trampoline?

RACHEL: Yes, oh, je vous aime beaucoup, trampoline.

NASSER: Speak my language, dammit.

RACHEL: I do nothing else. Nasser, d'you think we'll ever part?

NASSER: Not at the moment.

 (*Slapping her arse*) Keep moving, I love you. You move . . . Christ . . . like a liner . . .

RACHEL: And can't we go away somewhere?

NASSER: Yes, I'm taking you.

RACHEL: Where?

NASSER: Kempton Park, Saturday.

RACHEL: Great. We'll take the boy.

NASSER: No, I've got big plans for him.

RACHEL: You're going to make him work?

23.   INT. GARAGE OFFICE. DAY.

OMAR *has come into the garage office with his car-washing bucket and sponge.* SALIM *has gone home.* OMAR *is listening at the door to his uncle* NASSER *and* RACHEL *screwing. He hears:*

NASSER: Work? That boy? You'll think the word was invented for him!

24.   INT. COCKTAIL BAR/CLUB. EVENING.

RACHEL *and* NASSER *have taken* OMAR *to Anwar's club/bar.* OMAR *watches Anwar's son* TARIQ *behind the bar.* TARIQ *is rather contemptuous of* OMAR *and listens to their conversation.*

 OMAR *eats peanuts and olives off the bar.* TARIQ *removes the bowl.*

NASSER: By the way, Rachel is my old friend. (*To her.*) Eh?

OMAR: (*To* NASSER) How's Auntie Bilquis?

NASSER: (*Glancing at amused* RACHEL) She's at home with the kids.

OMAR: Papa sends his love. Uncle, if I picked Papa up –

NASSER: (*Indicating the club*) Have you been to a high-class place like this before? I suppose you stay in that black-hole flat all the time.

OMAR: If I picked Papa up, uncle –

NASSER: (*To* RACHEL) He's one of those underprivileged types.

OMAR: And squeezed him, squeezed Papa out, like that, uncle, I often imagine. I'd get –

NASSER: Two fat slaps.

OMAR: Two bottles of pure vodka. And a kind of flap of skin. (*To* RACHEL.) Like a French letter.

NASSER: What are you talking, madman? I love my brother. And I love you.

OMAR: I don't understand how you can . . . love me.

NASSER: Because you're such a prick?

OMAR: You can't be sure that I am.

RACHEL: Nasser.

NASSER: She's right. Don't deliberately egg me on to laugh at you when I've brought you here to tell you one essential thing. Move closer.

(OMAR *attempts to drag the stool he is sitting on near to* NASSER. *He crashes off it.* RACHEL *helps him up, laughing.* TARIQ *also laughs.* NASSER *is solicitous.*)

In this damn country which we hate and love, you can get anything you want. It's all spread out and available. That's why I believe in England. You just have to know how to squeeze the tits of the system.

RACHEL: (*To* OMAR) He's saying he wants to help you.

OMAR: What are you going to do with me?

NASSER: What am I going to do with you? Make you into something damn good. Your father can't now, can he?

(RACHEL *nods at* NASSER *and he takes out his wallet. He gives* OMAR *money.* OMAR *doesn't want to take it.* NASSER *shoves it down Omar's jumper, then cuddles his confused nephew.*)

57

Damn fool, you're just like a son to me. (*Looking at*
RACHEL.) To both of us.

25.   INT. GARAGE. DAY.

OMAR *is vigorously washing down a car, the last to be cleaned in the
garage. The other cars are gleaming.* NASSER *comes quickly out of
the office and watches* OMAR *squeezing a cloth over a bucket.*

NASSER: You like this work? (OMAR *shrugs.*) Come on, for
    Christ's sake, take a look at these accounts for me.
    (OMAR *follows him into the garage office.*)

26.   INT. GARAGE OFFICE. NIGHT.

OMAR *is sitting at the office desk in his shirt-sleeves. The desk is
covered with papers. He's been sitting there some time and it is late.
Most of the cars in the garage have gone.*

   NASSER *drives into the garage, wearing evening clothes.* RACHEL,
looking divine, is with him. OMAR *goes out to them.*

27.   INT. GARAGE. NIGHT.

NASSER: (*From the car*) Kiss Rachel. (OMAR *kisses her.*)
OMAR: I'll finish the paperwork tonight, Uncle.
NASSER: (*To* RACHEL) He's such a good worker I'm going to
    promote him.
RACHEL: What to?
NASSER: (*To* OMAR) Come to my house next week and I'll tell you.
RACHEL: It's far. How will he get there?
NASSER: I'll give him a car, dammit. (*He points to an old
    convertible parked in the garage. It has always looked out of
    place.*) The keys are in the office. Anything he wants. (*He
    moves the car off. To* OMAR.) Oh yes, I've got a real
    challenge lined up for you.
    (RACHEL *blows him a kiss as they drive off.*)

28.   INT. PAPA'S FLAT. EVENING.

PAPA *is lying on the bed drinking.* OMAR, *in new clothes, tie
undone, comes into the room and puts a plate of steaming food next to*
PAPA. *Stew and potatoes.* OMAR *turns away and looking in the
mirror snips at the hair in his nostrils with a large pair of scissors.*

PAPA: You must be getting married. Why else would you be dressed like an undertaker on holiday?

OMAR: Going to uncle's house, Papa. He's given me a car.

PAPA: What? The brakes must be faulty. Tell me one thing because there's something I don't understand, though it must be my fault. How is it that scrubbing cars can make a son of mine look so ecstatic?

OMAR: It gets me out of the house.

PAPA: Don't get too involved with that crook. You've got to study. We are under siege by the white man. For us education is power.

(OMAR *shakes his head at his father.*)

Don't let me down.

29. EXT. COUNTRY LANE. EVENING.

OMAR, *in the old convertible, speeds along a country lane in Kent. The car has its roof down, although it's raining. Loud music playing on the radio.*

He turns into the drive of a large detached house. The house is brightly lit. There are seven or eight cars in the drive. OMAR *sits there a moment, music blaring.*

30. INT. LIVING ROOM IN NASSER'S HOUSE. EVENING.

A large living room furnished in the modern style. A shy OMAR *has been led in by* BILQUIS, *Nasser's wife. She is a shy, middle-aged Pakistani woman. She speaks and understands English, but is uncertain in the language. But she is warm and friendly.*

OMAR *has already been introduced to most of the women in the room.*

There are five women there: a selection of wives; plus Bilquis's three daughters. The eldest, TANIA, *is in her early twenties.*

CHERRY, *Salim's Anglo-Indian wife is there.*

Some of the women are wearing saris or salwar kamiz, though not necessarily only the Pakistani women.

TANIA *wears jeans and T-shirt. She watches* OMAR *all through this and* OMAR, *when he can, glances at her. She is attracted to him.*

BILQUIS: (*To* OMAR) And this is Salim's wife, Cherry. And of course you remember our three naughty daughters.

59

CHERRY: (*Ebulliently to* BILQUIS) He has his family's
cheekbones, Bilquis. (*To* OMAR.) I know all your gorgeous
family in Karachi.

OMAR: (*This is a faux pas*) You've been there?

CHERRY: You stupid, what a stupid, it's my home. Could
anyone in their right mind call this silly little island off
Europe their home? Every day in Karachi, every day your
other uncles and cousins are at our house for bridge, booze
and VCR.

BILQUIS: Cherry, my little nephew knows nothing of that life
there.

CHERRY: Oh God, I'm so sick of hearing about these
in-betweens. People should make up their minds where
they are.

TANIA: Uncle's next door. (*Leading him away. Quietly.*) Can you
see me later? I'm so bored with these people.
(CHERRY *stares at* TANIA, *not approving of this whispering
and cousin-closeness.* TANIA *glares back defiantly at her.*
BILQUIS *looks warmly at* OMAR.)

31.   INT. CORRIDOR OF NASSER'S HOUSE. DAY.
TANIA *takes* OMAR *by the hand down the corridor to Nasser's room.*
She opens the door and leads him in.

32.   INT. NASSER'S ROOM. EVENING.
*Nasser's room is further down the corridor. It's his bedroom but
where he receives guests. And he has a VCR in the room, a fridge,
small bar, etc. Behind his bed a window which overlooks the garden.*
  OMAR *goes into the smoke-filled room, led by* TANIA. *She goes.*
  NASSER *is lying on his bed in the middle of the room like a fat
king. His cronies are gathered round the bed.* ZAKI, SALIM, *an*
ENGLISHMAN *and an American called* DICK O'DONNELL.
  They're shouting and hooting and boozing and listening to
NASSER's *story, which he tells with great energy.* OMAR *stands
inside the door shyly, and takes in the scene.*

NASSER: There'd been some tappings on the window. But who
would stay in a hotel without tappings? My brother
Hussein, the boy's papa, in his usual way hadn't turned up

60

and I was asleep. I presumed he was screwing some barmaid somewhere. Then when these tappings went on I got out of bed and opened the door to the balcony. And there he was, standing outside. With some woman! They were completely without clothes! And blue with cold! They looked like two bars of soap. This I refer to as my brother's blue period.

DICK O'DONNELL: What happened to the woman?

NASSER: He married her.

(*When* NASSER *notices the boy, conversation ceases with a wave of his hand. And* NASSER *unembarrassedly calls him over to be fondled and patted.*) Come along, come along. Your father's a good man.

DICK O'DONNELL: This is the famous Hussein's son?

NASSER: The exact bastard. My blue brother was also a famous journalist in Bombay and great drinker. He was to the bottle what Louis Armstrong is to the trumpet.

SALIM: But you are to the bookie what Mother Theresa is to the children.

ZAKI: (*To* NASSER) Your brother was the clever one. You used to carry his typewriter.

(TANIA *appears at the window behind the bed, where no one sees her but* OMAR *and then* ZAKI. *Later in the scene, laughing and to distract the serious-faced* OMAR, *she bares her breasts.* ZAKI *sees this and cannot believe his swimming-in-drink eyes.*)

DICK O'DONNELL: Isn't he coming tonight?

SALIM: (*To* NASSER) Whatever happened to him?

OMAR: Papa's lying down.

SALIM: I meant his career.

NASSER: That's lying down too. What chance would the Englishman give a leftist communist Pakistani on newspapers?

OMAR: Socialist. Socialist.

NASSER: What chance would the Englishman give a leftist communist socialist?

ZAKI: What chance has the racist Englishman given us that we haven't torn from him with our hands? Let's face up to it. (*And* ZAKI *has seen the breasts of* TANIA. *He goes white and panics.*)

61

NASSER: Zaki, have another stiff drink for that good point!

ZAKI: Nasser, please God, I am on the verge already!

ENGLISHMAN: Maybe Omar's father didn't make chances for himself. Look at you, Salim, five times richer and more powerful than me.

SALIM: Five times? Ten, at least.

ENGLISHMAN: In my country! The only prejudice in England is against the useless.

SALIM: It's rather tilted in favour of the useless I would think. The only positive discrimination they have here.

(*The* PAKISTANIS *in the room laugh at this. The* ENGLISHMAN *looks annoyed.* DICK O'DONNELL *smiles sympathetically at the* ENGLISHMAN.)

DICK O'DONNELL: (*To* NASSER) Can I make this nice boy a drink?

NASSER: Make him a man first.

SALIM: (*To* ZAKI) Give him a drink. I like him. He's our future.

33. INT. THE VERANDAH. NIGHT.

OMAR *shuts the door of Nasser's room and walks down the hall, to a games room at the end. This is a verandah overlooking the garden. There's a table-tennis table, various kids' toys, an exercise cycle, some cane chairs and on the walls numerous photographs of India.*

TANIA *turns as he enters and goes eagerly to him, touching him warmly.*

TANIA: It's been years. And you're looking good now. I bet we understand each other, eh?

(*He can't easily respond to her enthusiasm. Unoffended, she swings away from him. He looks at photographs of his Papa and Bhutto on the wall.*)

Are they being cruel to you in their typical men's way? (*He shrugs.*) You don't mind?

OMAR: I think I should harden myself.

TANIA: (*Patting seat next to her*) Wow, what are you into?

OMAR: Your father's done well.

(*He sits. She kisses him on the lips. They hold each other.*)

TANIA: Has he? He adores you. I expect he wants you to take over the businesses. He wouldn't think of asking me. But

he is too vicious to people in his work. He doesn't want you
to work in that shitty laundrette, does he?

OMAR: What's wrong with it?

TANIA: And he has a mistress, doesn't he?

(OMAR *looks up and sees* AUNTIE BILQUIS *standing at the
door.* TANIA *doesn't see her.*)

Rachel. Yes, I can tell from your face. Does he love her?
Yes. Families, I hate families.

BILQUIS: Please Tania, can you come and help.

(BILQUIS *goes.* TANIA *follows her.*)

34. INT. HALL OF NASSER'S HOUSE. DAY.

OMAR *is standing in the hall of Nasser's house as the guests leave
their respective rooms and go out into the drive.* OMAR *stands there.*
NASSER *shouts to him from his bed.*

NASSER: Take my advice. There's money in muck.

(TANIA *signals and shakes her head.*)

What is it the gora Englishman always needs? Clean clothes!

35. EXT. NASSER'S DRIVE. NIGHT.

OMAR *has come out of the house and into the drive. A strange sight:*
SALIM *staggering about drunkenly. The* ENGLISHMAN, ZAKI *and*
CHERRY *try to get him into the car.* SALIM *screams at* ZAKI.

SALIM: Don't you owe me money? Why not? You usually owe
me money! Here, take this! Borrow it! (*And he starts to
scatter money about.*) Pick it up!

(ZAKI *starts picking it up. He is afraid.*)

CHERRY: (*To* OMAR) Drive us back, will you. Pick up your own
car tomorrow. Salim is not feeling well.

(*As* ZAKI *bends over,* SALIM *who is laughing, goes to kick him.*
BILQUIS *stands at the window watching all this.*)

36. INT. SALIM'S CAR, DRIVING INTO SOUTH LONDON.
NIGHT.

OMAR *driving* SALIM's *car enthusiastically into London.* CHERRY
and SALIM *are in the back. The car comes to a stop at traffic lights.*

  On the adjacent pavement outside a chip shop a group of LADS *are
kicking cans about. The* LADS *include* MOOSE *and* GENGHIS.

A lively street of the illuminated shops, amusement arcades and late-night shops of South London.

MOOSE *notices that Pakistanis are in the car. And he indicates to the others.*

The LADS *gather round the car and bang on it and shout. From inside the car this noise is terrifying.* CHERRY *starts to scream.*

SALIM: Drive, you bloody fool, drive!

> (*But* MOOSE *climbs on the bonnet of the car and squashes his arse grotesquely against the windscreen. Faces squash against the other windows.*
>
> *Looking out of the side window* OMAR *sees* JOHNNY *standing to one side of the car, not really part of the car-climbing and banging.*
>
> *Impulsively, unafraid,* OMAR *gets out of the car.*)

37. EXT. STREET. NIGHT.

OMAR *walks past* GENGHIS *and* MOOSE *and the others to the embarrassed* JOHNNY. CHERRY *is yelling after him from inside the open-doored car.*

The LADS *are alert and ready for violence but are confused by* OMAR's *obvious friendship with* JOHNNY.

OMAR *sticks out his hand and* JOHNNY *takes it.*

OMAR: It's me.

JOHNNY: I know who it is.

OMAR: How are yer? Working? What you doing now then?

JOHNNY: Oh, this kinda thing.

CHERRY: (*Yelling from the car*) Come on, come on!

> (*The* LADS *laugh at her.* SALIM *is hastily giving* MOOSE *cigarettes.*)

JOHNNY: What are you now, chauffeur?

OMAR: No. I'm on to something.

JOHNNY: What?

OMAR: I'll let you know. Still living in the same place?

JOHNNY: Na, don't get on with me mum and dad. You?

OMAR: She died last year, my mother. Jumped on to the railway line.

JOHNNY: Yeah. I heard. All the trains stopped.

OMAR: I'm still there. Got the number?

64

JOHNNY: (*Indicates the* LADS) Like me friends?

    (CHERRY *starts honking the car horn. The* LADS *cheer.*)

OMAR: Ring us then.

JOHNNY: I will. (*Indicates car.*) Leave 'em there. We can do something. Now. Just us.

OMAR: Can't.

    (OMAR *touches* JOHNNY'S *arm and runs back to the car.*)

38.   INT. CAR. NIGHT.

They continue to drive. CHERRY *is screaming at* OMAR.

CHERRY: What the hell were you doing?

    (SALIM *slaps her.*)

SALIM: He saved our bloody arses! (*To* OMAR, *grabbing him round the neck and pressing his face close to his.*) I'm going to see you're all right!

39.   INT. PAPA'S ROOM. NIGHT.

OMAR *has got home. He creeps into the flat. He goes carefully along the hall, fingertips on familiar wall.*

   He goes into Papa's room. No sign of PAPA. PAPA *is on the balcony. Just a shadow.*

40.   EXT. BALCONY. NIGHT.

PAPA *is swaying on the balcony like a little tree. Papa's pyjama bottoms have fallen down. And he's just about maintaining himself vertically. His hair has fallen across his terrible face. A train bangs towards him, rushing out of the darkness. And* PAPA *sways precariously towards it.*

OMAR: (*Screams above the noise*) What are you doing?

PAPA: I want to pee.

OMAR: Can't you wait for me to take you!

PAPA: My prick will drop off before you show up these days.

OMAR: (*Pulling up Papa's bottoms*) You know who I met? Johnny. Johnny.

PAPA: The boy who came here one day dressed as a fascist with a quarter inch of hair?

OMAR: He was a friend once. For years.

PAPA: There were days when he didn't deserve your admiration so much.

OMAR: Christ, I've known him since I was five.
PAPA: He went too far. They hate us in England. And all you do
is kiss their arses and think of yourself as a little Britisher!

41. INT. PAPA'S ROOM. NIGHT.
They are inside the room now, and OMAR *shuts the doors.*
OMAR: I'm being promoted. To uncle's laundrette.
(PAPA *pulls a pair of socks from his pyjama pockets and thrusts
them at* OMAR.)
PAPA: Illustrate your washing methods!
(OMAR *throws the socks across the room.*)

42. EXT. SOUTH LONDON STREET. DAY.
NASSER *and* OMAR *get out of Nasser's car and walk over the road to
the laundrette. It's called 'Churchills'. It's broad and spacious and in
bad condition. It's situated in an area of run-down second-hand
shops, betting shops, grocers with their windows boarded-up, etc.*
NASSER: It's nothing but a toilet and a youth club now. A finger
up my damn arse.

43. INT. LAUNDRETTE. DAY.
*We are inside the laundrette. Some of the benches in the laundrette
are church pews.*
OMAR: Where did you get those?
NASSER: Church.
(*Three or four rough-looking* KIDS, *boys and girls, one of whom
isn't wearing shoes, sitting on the pews. A character by the
telephone. The thunderous sound of running-shoes in a spin-drier.
The* KID *coolly opens the spin-drier and takes out his shoes.*)
Punkey, that's how machines get buggered!
(*The* KID *puts on his shoes. He offers his hot-dog to another*
KID, *who declines it. So the* KID *flings it into a spin-drier.*
   NASSER *moves to throttle him. He gets the* KID *by the throat.
The other* KIDS *get up.* OMAR *pulls his eager* UNCLE *away.
The* TELEPHONE CHARACTER *looks suspiciously at everyone.
Then makes his call.*)
TELEPHONE CHARACTER: Hi, baby, it's number one here,
baby. How's your foot now?

44. INT. BACK ROOM OF LAUNDRETTE. DAY.

NASSER *stands at the desk going through bills and papers.*

NASSER: (*To* OMAR) Get started. There's the broom. Move it!

OMAR: I don't only want to sweep up.

NASSER: What are you now, Labour Party?

OMAR: I want to be manager of this place. I think I can do it.
(*Pause.*) Please let me.
(NASSER *thinks.*)

NASSER: I'm just thinking how to tell your father that four
punks drowned you in a washing machine. On the other
hand, some water on the brain might clear your thoughts.
Okay. Pay me a basic rent. Above that – you keep.
(*He goes quickly, eager to get out. The* TELEPHONE
CHARACTER *is shouting into the phone.*)

TELEPHONE CHARACTER: (*Into phone*) Was it my fault? But
you're everything to me! More than everything. I prefer
you to Janice!
(*The* TELEPHONE CHARACTER *indicates to* NASSER *that a
washing machine has overflowed all over the floor, with
soap suds.* NASSER *gets out.* OMAR *looks on.*)

45. INT. BACK ROOM OF LAUNDRETTE. DAY.

OMAR *sitting gloomily in the back room. The door to the main area
open.* KIDS *push each other about. Straight customers are
intimidated.*

From Omar's POV through the laundrette windows, we see
SALIM *getting out of his car.* SALIM *walks in through the laundrette,
quickly. Comes into the back room, slamming the door behind him.*

SALIM: Get up! (OMAR *gets up.* SALIM *rams the back of a chair
under the door handle.*) I've had trouble here.

OMAR: Salim, please. I don't know how to make this place
work. I'm afraid I've made a fool of myself.

SALIM: You'll never make a penny out of this. Your uncle's
given you a dead duck. That's why I've decided to help you
financially. (*He gives him a piece of paper with an address on
it. He also gives him money.*) Go to this house near the
airport. Pick up some video cassettes and bring them to my
flat. That's all.

46. INT. SALIM'S FLAT. EVENING.

The flat is large and beautiful. Some Sindi music playing. SALIM
*comes out of the bathroom wearing only a towel round his waist. And
a plastic shower cap. He is smoking a fat joint.*

    CHERRY *goes into another room.*

    OMAR *stands there with the cassettes in his arms.* SALIM *indicates
them.*

SALIM: Put them. Relax. No problems? (SALIM *gives him the
    joint and* OMAR *takes a hit on it.* SALIM *points at the walls.
    Some erotic and some very good paintings.*) One of the best
    collections of recent Indian painting. I patronize many
    painters. I won't be a minute. Watch something if you like.
    (SALIM *goes back into the bedroom.* OMAR *puts one of the
    cassettes he has brought into the VCR. But there's nothing on
    the tape. Just a screenful of static.*

       Meanwhile, OMAR *makes a call, taking the number off a
    piece of paper.*)

OMAR: (*Into phone*) Can I speak to Johnny? D'you know where
    he's staying? Are you sure? Just wanted to help him.
    Please, if you see him, tell him to ring Omo.

47. INT. SALIM'S FLAT. EVENING.

Dressed now, and ready to go out, SALIM *comes quickly into the
room. He picks up the video cassettes and realizes one is being
played.* SALIM *screams savagely at* OMAR.

SALIM: Is that tape playing? (OMAR *nods.*) What the hell are you
    doing? (*He pulls the tape out of the VCR and examines it.*)

OMAR: Just watching something, Salim.

SALIM: Not these! Who gave you permission to touch these?
    (OMAR *grabs the tape from* SALIM'*s hand.*)

OMAR: It's just a tape!

SALIM: Not to me!

OMAR: What are you doing? What business, Salim?
    (SALIM *pushes* OMAR *hard and* OMAR *crashes backwards
    across the room. As he gets up quickly to react* SALIM *is at him,
    shoving him back down, viciously. He puts his foot on* OMAR'*s
    nose.*

       CHERRY *watches him coolly, leaning against a door jamb.*)

SALIM: Nasser tells me you're ambitious to do something. But twice you failed your exams. You've done nothing with the laundrette and now you bugger me up. You've got too much white blood. It's made you weak like those pale-faced adolescents that call us wog. You know what I do to them? I take out this. (*He takes out a pound note. He tears it to pieces.*) I say: your English pound is worthless. It's worthless like you, Omar, are worthless. Your whole great family – rich and powerful over there – is let down by you.
(OMAR *gets up slowly.*)
Now fuck off.

OMAR: I'll do something to you for this.

SALIM: I'd be truly happy to see you try.

48. EXT. OUTSIDE LAUNDRETTE. EVENING.
OMAR, *depressed after his humiliation at* SALIM's, *drives slowly past the laundrette. Music plays over this. It's raining and the laundrette looks grim and hopeless.*
    OMAR *sees* GENGHIS *and* MOOSE. *He drives up alongside them.*

OMAR: Seen Johnny?

GENGHIS: Get back to the jungle, wog boy.
    (MOOSE *kicks the side of the car.*)

49. INT. PAPA'S ROOM. EVENING.
OMAR *is cutting* PAPA's *long toenails with a large pair of scissors.*
OMAR's *face is badly bruised.* PAPA *jerks about, pouring himself a drink. So* OMAR *has to keep grabbing at his feet. The skin on* PAPA's *legs is peeling through lack of vitamins.*

PAPA: Those people are too tough for you. I'll tell Nasser you're through with them. (PAPA *dials. We hear it ringing in Nasser's house. He puts the receiver to one side to pick up his drink. He looks at* OMAR *who wells with anger and humiliation.* TANIA *answers.*)

TANIA: Hallo.
    (OMAR *moves quickly and breaks the connection.*)

PAPA: (*Furious*) Why do that, you useless fool?
    (OMAR *grabs* PAPA's *foot and starts on the toe job again. The phone starts to ring.* PAPA *pulls away and* OMAR *jabs him with the scissors. And* PAPA *bleeds.* OMAR *answers the phone.*)

69

OMAR: Hallo. (*Pause.*) Johnny.

PAPA: (*Shouts over*) I'll throw you out of this bloody flat, you're nothing but a bum liability!

(*But* OMAR *is smiling into the phone and talking to* JOHNNY, *a finger in one ear.*)

50.   INT. THE LAUNDRETTE. DAY.

OMAR *is showing* JOHNNY *round the laundrette.*

JOHNNY: I'm dead impressed by all this.

OMAR: You were the one at school. The one they liked.

JOHNNY: (*Sarcastic*) All the Pakis liked me.

OMAR: I've been through it. With my parents and that. And with people like you. But now there's some things I want to do. Some pretty big things I've got in mind. I need to raise money to make this place good. I want you to help me do that. And I want you to work here with me.

JOHNNY: What kinda work is it?

OMAR: Variety. Variety of menial things.

JOHNNY: Cleaning windows kinda thing, yeah?

OMAR: Yeah. Sure. And clean out those bastards, will ya?

(OMAR *indicates the sitting* KIDS *playing about on the benches.*)

JOHNNY: Now?

OMAR: I'll want everything done now. That's the only attitude if you want to do anything big.

(JOHNNY *goes to the* KIDS *and stands above them. Slowly he removes his watch and puts it in his pocket. This is a strangely threatening gesture. The* KIDS *rise and walk out one by one. One* KID *resents this. He pushes* JOHNNY *suddenly.* JOHNNY *kicks him hard.*)

51.   EXT. OUTSIDE THE LAUNDRETTE. DAY.

Continuous. The kicked KID *shoots across the pavement and crashes into* SALIM *who is getting out of his car.* SALIM *pushes away the frantic arms and legs and goes quickly into the laundrette.*

52.   INT. LAUNDRETTE. DAY.

SALIM *drags the reluctant* OMAR *by the arm into the back room of the laundrette.* JOHNNY *watches them, then follows.*

53.   INT. BACK ROOM OF LAUNDRETTE. DAY.

SALIM *lets go of* OMAR *and grabs a chair to stuff under the door handle as before.* OMAR *suddenly snatches the chair from him and puts it down slowly. And* JOHNNY, *taking* OMAR's *lead, sticks his big boot in the door as* SALIM *attempts to slam it.*

SALIM: Christ, Omar, sorry what happened before. Too much to drink. Just go on one little errand for me, eh? (*He opens* OMAR's *fingers and presses a piece of paper into his hand.*) Like before. For me.

OMAR: For fifty quid as well.

SALIM: You little bastard.

(OMAR *turns away.* JOHNNY *turns away too, mocking* SALIM, *parodying* OMAR.)

All right.

54.   INT. HOTEL ROOM. DUSK.

OMAR *is standing in a hotel room. A modern high building with a view over London. He is with a middle-aged Pakistani who is wearing salwar kamiz. Suitcases on the floor.*

The MAN *has a long white beard. Suddenly he peels it off and hands it to* OMAR. OMAR *is astonished. The* MAN *laughs uproariously.*

55.   INT. LAUNDRETTE. EVENING.

JOHNNY *is doing a service wash in the laundrette.* OMAR *comes in quickly, the beard in a plastic bag. He puts the beard on.*

JOHNNY: You fool.

(OMAR *pulls* JOHNNY *towards the back room.*)

OMAR: I've sussed Salim's game. This is going to finance our whole future.

56.   INT. BACK ROOM OF LAUNDRETTE. DAY.

JOHNNY *and* OMAR *sitting at the desk.* JOHNNY *is unpicking the back of the beard with a pair of scissors. The door to the laundrette is closed.*

JOHNNY *carefully pulls plastic bags out of the back of the beard. He looks enquiringly at* OMAR. OMAR *confidently indicates that he should open one of them.* JOHNNY *looks doubtfully at him.* OMAR

71

pulls the chair closer. JOHNNY *snips a corner off the bag. He*
opens it and tastes the powder on his finger. He nods at OMAR.
JOHNNY *quickly starts stuffing the bags back in the beard.*
  OMAR *gets up.*

OMAR: Take them out. You know where to sell this stuff. Yes?
    Don't you?

JOHNNY: I wouldn't be working for you now if I wanted to go
    on being a bad boy.

OMAR: This means more. Real work. Expansion.
    (JOHNNY *reluctantly removes the rest of the packets from the*
    back of the beard.)
    We'll re-sell it fast. Tonight.

JOHNNY: Salim'll kill us.

OMAR: Why should he find out it's us? Better get this back to
    him. Come on. I couldn't be doing any of this without you.

57. INT. OUTSIDE SALIM'S FLAT. NIGHT.
OMAR, *wearing the beard, is standing outside* SALIM's *flat, having*
rung the bell. CHERRY *answers the door. At first she doesn't*
recognize him. Then he laughs. And she pulls him in.

58. INT. SALIM'S FLAT. NIGHT.
There are ten people sitting in SALIM's *flat. Well-off Pakistani*
friends who have come round for dinner. They are chatting and
drinking. At the other end of the room the table has been laid for
dinner.
  SALIM *is fixing drinks, and talking to his friends over his*
shoulder.

SALIM: We were all there, yaar, to see Ravi Shankar. But you all
    just wanted to talk about my paintings. My collection.
    That's why I said, why don't you all come round. I will
    turn my place into an art gallery for the evening . . . (*The*
    friends are giggling at OMAR, *who is wearing the beard.*
    SALIM, *disturbed, turns suddenly.* SALIM *is appalled by* OMAR
    in the beard.) Let's have a little private chat, eh?

59. INT. SALIM'S BEDROOM. EVENING.
SALIM *snatches the beard from* OMAR's *chin. He goes into the*

72

bathroom with it. OMAR *moves towards the bathroom and watches*
SALIM *frantically examine the back of the beard. When* SALIM *sees,
in the mirror,* OMAR *watching him, he kicks the door shut.*

60.   INT. SALIM'S BEDROOM. NIGHT.
SALIM *comes back into the bedroom from the bathroom. He throws
down the beard.*
SALIM: You can go.
OMAR: But you haven't paid me.
SALIM: I'm not in the mood. Nothing happened to you on the
    way here? (OMAR *shakes his head.*) Well, something may
    happen to you on the way back. (SALIM *is unsure at the
    moment what's happened.* OMAR *watches him steadily. His
    nerve is holding out.*) Get the hell out.

61.   EXT. OUTSIDE SALIM'S FLAT. NIGHT.
As OMAR *runs down the steps of the flats to* JOHNNY *waiting in the
revving car,* SALIM *stands at the window of his flat, watching them.
Music over. We go with the music into:*

62.   INT. CLUB/BAR. NIGHT.
OMAR *has taken* JOHNNY *to the club he visited with* NASSER *and*
RACHEL.
   *The club is more lively in the evening, with West Indian, English
and Pakistani customers. All affluent. In fact, a couple of the*
JAMAICANS *from the opening scene are there.*
   OMAR *and* JOHNNY *are sitting at a table.* TARIQ, *the young son
of the club's owner, stands beside them. He puts two menus down.*
TARIQ: (*To* OMAR) Of course a table is always here for you.
    Your Uncle Nasser – a great man. And Salim, of course. No
    one touches him. No one. You want to eat?
OMAR: Tariq, later. Bring us champagne first. (TARIQ *goes. To*
    JOHNNY.) Okay?
JOHNNY: I'm selling the stuff tonight. The bloke's coming here
    in an hour. He's testing it now.
OMAR: Good. (*Smiles at a girl.*) She's nice.
JOHNNY: Yes.

73

63.   INT. CLUB/BAR. NIGHT.

OMAR *is sitting alone at the table, drinking.* TARIQ *clears the table and goes.* JOHNNY *comes out of the toilet with the white* DEALER. *The* DEALER *goes.* JOHNNY *goes and sits beside* OMAR.

JOHNNY: We're laughing.

64.   INT. NASSER'S ROOM. EVENING.

NASSER *is lying on his bed wearing salwar kamiz. One of the young* DAUGHTERS *is pressing his legs and he groans with delight.* OMAR *is sitting across the room from him, well-dressed and relaxed. He eats Indian sweets. The other* DAUGHTER *comes in with more sweets, which she places by* OMAR.

OMAR: Tell me about the beach at Bombay, Uncle. Juhu beach.
> (*But* NASSER *is in a bad mood.* TANIA *comes into the room. She is wearing salwar kamiz for the first time in the film. And she looks stunning. She has dressed up for* OMAR.)
> (*Playing to* TANIA) Or the house in Lahore. When Auntie Nina put the garden hose in the window of my father's bedroom because he wouldn't get up. And Papa's bed started to float.
> (TANIA *stands behind* OMAR *and touches him gently on the shoulder. She is laughing at the story.*)

TANIA: Papa.
> (*But he ignores her.*)

OMAR: (*To* TANIA) You look beautiful.
> (*She squeezes his arm.*)

NASSER: (*Sitting up suddenly*) What about my damn laundrette? Damn these stories about a place you've never been. What are you doing, boy!

OMAR: What am I doing?

65.   INT. LAUNDRETTE. DAY.

OMAR *and* JOHNNY *in the laundrette.* JOHNNY, *with an axe, is smashing one of the broken-down benches off the wall while* OMAR *stands there surveying the laundrette, pencil and pad in hand. Splinters, bits of wood fly about as* JOHNNY, *athletically and enthusiastically singing at the top of his voice, demolishes existing structures.*

OMAR: (*Voice over*) It'll be going into profit any day now. Partly

74

because I've hired a bloke of outstanding competence and
strength of body and mind to look after it with me.

66.   INT. NASSER'S ROOM. EVENING.
NASSER: (*To young* DAUGHTER) Jasmine, fiddle with my toes.
(*To* OMAR) What bloke?

67.   INT. LAUNDRETTE. DAY.
JOHNNY *is up a ladder vigorously painting a wall and singing
loudly. The washing machines are covered with white sheets. Pots
and paints and brushes lie about.*
   OMAR *watches* JOHNNY.
OMAR: (*Voice over*) He's called Johnny.
NASSER: (*Voice over*) How will you pay him?

68.   INT. NASSER'S ROOM. EVENING.
SALIM *and* ZAKI *come into the room.* SALIM *carries a bottle of
whisky.* ZAKI *looks nervously at* TANIA *who flutters her eyelashes at
him.*
   SALIM *and* ZAKI *shake hands with* NASSER *and sit down in chairs
round the bed.*
ZAKI: (*To* NASSER) How are you, you old bastard?
NASSER: (*Pointing at drinks*) Tania.
      (TANIA *fixes drinks for everyone.* SALIM *looks suspiciously at*
      OMAR *through this. But* OMAR *coolly ignores him.*)
      Zaki, how's things now then?
ZAKI: Oh good, good, everything. But . . .
      (*He begins to explain about his declining laundrette business
      and how bad his heart is, in Urdu.* NASSER *waves at* OMAR.)
NASSER: Speak in English, Zaki, so this boy can understand.
ZAKI: He doesn't understand his own language?
NASSER: (*With affectionate mock anger*) Not only that. I've given
      him that pain-in-the-arse laundrette to run.
SALIM: I know.
NASSER: But this is the point. He's hired someone else to do the
      work!
ZAKI: Typically English, if I can say that.
SALIM: (*Harshly*) Don't fuck your uncle's business, you little fool.

TANIA: I don't think you should talk to him like that, Uncle.

SALIM: Why, what is he, royalty?

(SALIM *and* NASSER *exchange amused looks*.)

ZAKI: (*To* NASSER) She is a hot girl.

TANIA: I don't like it.

OMAR: (*To* SALIM) In my small opinion, much good can come
of fucking.

(TANIA *laughs*. ZAKI *is shocked*. SALIM *stares at* OMAR.)

NASSER: (*To* OMAR) Your mouth is getting very big lately.

OMAR: Well. (*And he gets up quickly, to walk out*.)

NASSER: All right, all right, let's all take it easy.

SALIM: Who is it sitting in the drive? It's bothering me.
(*To* TANIA.) Some friend of yours?
(*She shakes her head*.)

NASSER: Zaki, go and check it for me please.

OMAR: It's only Johnny. My friend. He works for me.

NASSER: No one works without my permission.
(*To* TANIA.) Bring him here now.
(*She goes*. OMAR *gets up and follows her*.)

69.   EXT. NASSER'S FRONT DRIVE. EVENING.

JOHNNY *is standing by the car, music coming from the car radio*.
TANIA *and* OMAR *walk over to him*. TANIA *takes* OMAR's *arm*.

TANIA: I know why you put up with them. Because there's so
much you want. You're greedy like my father. (*Nodding
towards* JOHNNY.) Why did you leave him out here?

OMAR: He's lower class. He won't come in without being asked.
Unless he's doing a burglary.
(*They get to* JOHNNY, OMAR *not minding if he overhears the
last remark*.)

TANIA: Come in, Johnny. My father's waiting for you.
(*She turns and walks away*. OMAR *and* JOHNNY *walk
towards the house*. BILQUIS *is standing in the window of
the front room, looking at them*. OMAR *smiles and waves at
her*.)

JOHNNY: How's Salim today?

OMAR: Wearing too much perfume as usual. (OMAR *stops*
JOHNNY *a moment and brushes his face*.) An eyelash.

76

(TANIA, *waiting at the door, watches this piece of affection and wonders.*)

70. INT. NASSER'S ROOM. EVENING.

NASSER, SALIM, JOHNNY, ZAKI *and* OMAR *are laughing together at one of Nasser's stories.* JOHNNY *has been introduced and they are getting along well.* TANIA *hands* SALIM *another drink and checks that everyone else has drinks.*

NASSER: . . . So I said, in my street I am the law! You see, I make wealth, I create money.

(*There is a slight pause.* NASSER *indicates to* TANIA *that she should leave the room. She does so, irritably.* SALIM *tries to take her hand as she goes but she pulls away from him. She has gone now.*)

(*To* OMAR) You like Tania?

OMAR: Oh yes.

NASSER: I'll see what I can do.

(ZAKI *laughs and slaps* OMAR *on the knee.* OMAR *is uncomprehending.*)

To business now. I went to see the laundrette. You boys will make a beautiful job of it, I know. You need nothing more from there. (*To* JOHNNY.) But in exchange I want you to do something. You look like a tough chap. I've got some bastard tenants in one of my houses I can't get rid of.

JOHNNY: No, I don't do nothing rough no more.

NASSER: I'm not looking for a mass murderer, you bloody fool.

JOHNNY: What's it involve, please?

NASSER: I tell you. Unscrewing. (*To* SALIM.) We're on your favourite subject.

SALIM: For Christ's sake!

JOHNNY: What is unscrewing?

ZAKI: You're getting into some family business, that's all.

SALIM: What the hell else is there for them in this country now?

NASSER: (*To* OMAR) Send him to my garage. And call Tania to bring us champagne. And we'll drink to Thatcher and your beautiful laundrette.

JOHNNY: Do they go together?

NASSER: Like dall and chipatis!

77

71. EXT. OUTSIDE THE LAUNDRETTE. NIGHT.

JOHNNY *and* OMAR *have parked their car by the laundrette. They lean against the car, close together, talking.*

JOHNNY: The timber's coming tomorrow morning. I'm getting it cheap.

(*They walk slowly towards the laundrette.*)

OMAR: I've had a vision. Of how this place could be. Why do people hate laundrettes? Because they're like toilets. This could be a Ritz among laundrettes.

JOHNNY: A laundrette as big as the Ritz. Yeah.

(JOHNNY *puts his arm round* OMAR. OMAR *turns to him and they kiss on the mouth. They kiss passionately and hold each other.*

On the other side of the laundrette, GENGHIS, MOOSE *and three other* LADS *are kicking the laundrette dustbins across the pavement. They can't see* OMAR *and* JOHNNY.

JOHNNY *detaches himself from* OMAR *and walks round the laundrette to the* LADS. OMAR *moves into a position from where he can see, but doesn't approach the* LADS.

MOOSE *sees* JOHNNY *and motions to* GENGHIS *who is engrossed with the kicking.* GENGHIS *faces* JOHNNY. JOHNNY *controls himself. He straightens the dustbin and starts banging the rubbish back in. He gestures to a couple of the* LADS *to help him. They move back, away from him.*

JOHNNY *grabs* MOOSE *by the hair and stuffs his head into a dustbin.* MOOSE, *suitably disciplined, then helps* JOHNNY *stuff the rubbish back in the bin, looking guiltily at* GENGHIS.)

GENGHIS: Why are you working for them? For these people? You were with us once. For England.

JOHNNY: It's work. I want to work. I'm fed up of hanging about.

GENGHIS: I'm angry. I don't like to see one of our men grovelling to Pakis. They came here to work for us. That's why we brought them over. OK?

(*And* GENGHIS *moves away. As he does so, he sees* OMAR. *The others see him at the same time.* MOOSE *takes out a knife.* GENGHIS *indicates for him to keep back. He wants to concentrate on* JOHNNY.)

78

Don't cut yourself off from your own people. Because
there's no one else who really wants you. Everyone
has to belong.

72.   EXT. SOUTH LONDON STREET. NIGHT.
*They are in a street of desolate semi-detached houses in bad
condition, ready for demolition.* JOHNNY *kisses* OMAR *and opens the
car door.*
JOHNNY: I can't ask you in. And you'd better get back to your
    father.
OMAR: I didn't think you'd ever mention my father.
JOHNNY: He helped me, didn't he? When I was at school.
OMAR: And what did you do but hurt him?
JOHNNY: I want to forget all of those things.
    (*He gets out quickly and walks across the front of the car. He
    turns the corner of the street.* OMAR *gets out of the car and
    follows him.*)

73.   EXT. STREET. NIGHT.
OMAR *follows* JOHNNY, *making sure he isn't seen.*
    JOHNNY *turns into a boarded-up derelict house.* OMAR *watches
him go round the side of the house and climb in through a broken
door.*
    OMAR *turns away.*

74.   INT. PAPA'S FLAT. NIGHT.
PAPA *is asleep in the room, dead drunk and snoring.* OMAR *has
come in. He stands by Papa's bed and strokes his head.*
    *He picks up an almost empty bottle of vodka and drinks from it,
finishing it. He goes to the balcony door with it.*

75.   EXT. BALCONY. NIGHT.
OMAR *stands on the balcony, looking over the silent railway line.
Then, suddenly, he shouts joyfully into the distance. And throws the
empty bottle as far as he can.*

76.   EXT. OUTSIDE THE LAUNDRETTE. DAY.
OMAR *and* JOHNNY *are working hard and with great concentration,*

painting the outside of the laundrette, the doors, etc. Although it's not finished, it's beginning to reach its final state. The new windows have been installed; but the neon sign isn't yet up.

KIDS *play football nearby. And various cynical* LOCALS *watch, a couple of* OLD MEN *who we see in the betting shop later. Also* MOOSE *and another* LAD *who are amused by all the effort. They lean against a wall opposite and drink from cans.*

Further up the street SALIM *is watching all this from his parked car.*

JOHNNY *is up a ladder. He gets down the ladder, nods goodbye to* OMAR *and puts his paint brush away.* SALIM *reverses his car.*

JOHNNY *walks away.* OMAR *looks nervously across at* MOOSE *who stares at him.*

77. INT. GARAGE OFFICE. DAY.

NASSER *and* SALIM *in the glassed-in office of the garage.* NASSER *is going through various papers on his desk.* SALIM *watches him and is very persistent.*

SALIM: I passed by the laundrette. So you gave them money to do it up? (NASSER *shakes his head.*) Where did they get it from, I wonder?

NASSER: Government grant. (SALIM *looks dubiously at* NASSER.) Oh, Omo's like us, yaar. Doesn't he fit with us like a glove? He's pure bloody family. (*Looks knowingly at* SALIM.) So, like you, God knows what he's doing for money. (NASSER *looks up and sees* JOHNNY *squashing his face against the glass of the door of the office. He starts to laugh.*)

SALIM: That other joker's a bad influence on Omo. I'm sure of it. There's some things between them I'm looking into.
(JOHNNY *comes in.*)
(*To* JOHNNY) So they let you out of prison. Too crowded, are they?

JOHNNY: Unscrew.
(SALIM *reacts.* NASSER *quickly leads* JOHNNY *out of the office, while speaking to* SALIM *through the open door.*)

NASSER: (*In Urdu*) Don't worry, I'm just putting this bastard to work.

SALIM: (*In Urdu*) The bastard, it's a job in itself.

80

NASSER: (*In Urdu*) I'll have my foot up his arse at all times.
SALIM: (*In Urdu*) That's exactly how they like it. And he'll steal
　　　your boot too.
　　　(JOHNNY *looks amusedly at them both.*)

78.　INT. HOUSE. DAY.
*This is one of Nasser's properties. A falling down four-storey place in
South London, the rooms of which he rents out to itinerants and
students.*
　　　Peeling walls, faded carpets, cat piss. JOHNNY *and* NASSER *are
on the top landing of the house, standing by a door.* JOHNNY *is
holding a tool kit, which he starts to unpack.*
NASSER: He's changed the lock so you take off the whole door
　　　in case he changes it again. He's only a poet with no money.
JOHNNY: I'm not hurting nobody, OK?

79.　INT. TOP CORRIDOR OF HOUSE. DAY.
Later. NASSER *has gone.* JOHNNY *has got through the lock and the
door is open. He is unscrewing the hinges and singing to himself.*
　　　At the end of the hall a Pakistani in his fifties watches him.
JOHNNY *lifts the door off the frame and leans it against the wall.*
POET: Now that door you've just taken off. Hang it back.
　　　(*With great grunting effort* JOHNNY *picks the door up. He tries
　　　hard to move past the* POET *with it. The* POET *shoves* JOHNNY
　　　hard. JOHNNY *almost balances himself again but not quite,
　　　does a kind of dance with the door before crashing over with it
　　　on top of him.*
　　　　JOHNNY *struggles to his feet. The* POET *advances towards
　　　him and* JOHNNY *retreats.*)
　　　I'm a poor man. This is my room. Let's leave it that way.
　　　(*And the* POET *shoves* JOHNNY *again.*
　　　　JOHNNY, *not wanting to resist, falls against the wall.
　　　　At the end of the hall, at the top of the stairs,* NASSER
　　　appears. The* POET *turns to* NASSER *and moves towards him,
　　　abusing him in Punjabi.* NASSER *ignores him. As the* POET
　　　goes for* NASSER, JOHNNY *grabs the* POET *from behind and
　　　twists his arm up behind him.*)
NASSER: Throw this bugger out!

81

(JOHNNY *shoves the struggling* POET *along the corridor to the top of the stairs and then bundles him downstairs.*)

80. INT. ROOM. DAY.
The room from which JOHNNY *removed the door. A large badly furnished bedsit with a cooker, fridge, double-bed, wardrobe, etc.*
   NASSER *is giving* JOHNNY *money. Then* NASSER *opens the window and looks out down the street. The* POET *is walking away from the house.* NASSER *calls out after him in Punjabi. And he throws the poet's things out of the window. The* POET *scrabbles around down below, gathering his things.*)
JOHNNY: Aren't you giving ammunition to your enemies doing this kind of . . . unscrewing? To people who say Pakis just come here to hustle other people's lives and jobs and houses.
NASSER: But we're professional businessmen. Not professional Pakistanis. There's no race question in the new enterprise culture. Do you like the room? Omar said you had nowhere to live. I won't charge.
JOHNNY: Why not?
NASSER: You can unscrew. That's confirmed beautifully. But can you unblock and can you keep this zoo here under control? Eh?

81. EXT. LAUNDRETTE. EVENING.
Music.
   JOHNNY *is working on the outside of the laundrette. He's fixing up the neon sign, on his own, and having difficulty.* OMAR *stands down below, expensively dressed, not willing to assist. Across the street* MOOSE *and a couple of* LADS *are watching.*
OMAR: I wish Salim could see this.
JOHNNY: Why? He's on to us. Oh yeah, he's just biding his time. Then he'll get us.
   (*He indicates to* MOOSE. MOOSE *comes over and helps him.*
      The OLD MEN *are watching wisely as* JOHNNY *and* MOOSE *precariously sway on a board suspended across two ladders, while holding the neon sign saying* POWDERS.)
OMAR: You taking the room in Nasser's place?

(*A ball is kicked by the* KIDS *which whistles past* JOHNNY'*s ear.*
MOOSE *reacts.*)
Make sure you pay the rent. Otherwise you'll have to chuck
yourself out of the window.
(GENGHIS *walks down the street towards the laundrette.* OMAR
turns and goes.

   MOOSE *goes into a panic, knowing* GENGHIS *will be furious
at this act of collaboration.* JOHNNY *glances at* MOOSE.

   GENGHIS *is coming. The ladders sway. And the* OLD MEN
watch. GENGHIS *stops.* MOOSE *looks at him.*)

82. INT. LAUNDRETTE. DAY.
The day of the opening of the laundrette.

   *The laundrette is finished. And the place looks terrific: pot plants;
a TV on which videos are showing; a sound system; and the place is
brightly painted and clean.*

   OMAR *is splendidly dressed. He is walking round the place, drink
in hand, looking it over.*

   *Outside, local people look in curiously and press their faces
against the glass. Two old ladies are patiently waiting to be let in. A
queue of people with washing gradually forms.*

   In the open door of the back room JOHNNY *is changing into his
new clothes.*

JOHNNY: Let's open. The world's waiting.
OMAR: I've invited Nasser to the launch. And Papa's coming.
   They're not here yet. Papa hasn't been out for months. We
   can't move till he arrives.
JOHNNY: What time did they say they'd be here?
OMAR: An hour ago.
JOHNNY: They're not gonna come, then.
   (OMAR *looks hurt.* JOHNNY *indicates that* OMAR *should go to
   him. He goes to him.*)

83. INT. BACK ROOM OF LAUNDRETTE. DAY.
*The back room has also been done up, in a bright high-tech style.
And a two-way mirror has been installed, through which they can see
into the laundrette.*

   OMAR *watches* JOHNNY, *sitting on the desk.*

83

JOHNNY: Shall I open the champagne then? (*He opens the bottle.*)

OMAR: Didn't I predict this? (*They look through the mirror and through the huge windows of the laundrette to the patient punters waiting outside.*) This whole stinking area's on its knees begging for clean clothes. Jesus Christ.

(OMAR *touches his own shoulders.* JOHNNY *massages him.*)

JOHNNY: Let's open up.

OMAR: Not till Papa comes. Remember? He went out of his way with you. And with all my friends. (*Suddenly harsh.*) He did, didn't he!

JOHNNY: Omo. What are you on about, mate?

OMAR: About how years later he saw the same boys. And what were they doing?

JOHNNY: What?

OMAR: What were they doing on marches through Lewisham? It was bricks and bottles and Union Jacks. It was immigrants out. It was kill us. People we knew. And it was you. He saw you marching. You saw his face, watching you. Don't deny it. We were there when you went past. (OMAR *is being held by* JOHNNY, *in his arms.*) Papa hated himself and his job. He was afraid on the street for me. And he took it out on her. And she couldn't bear it. Oh, such failure, such emptiness.

(JOHNNY *kisses* OMAR *then leaves him, sitting away from him slightly.* OMAR *touches him, asking him to hold him.*)

84. INT. LAUNDRETTE. DAY.

NASSER *and* RACHEL *stride enthusiastically into the not yet open laundrette, carrying paper cups and a bottle of whisky. Modern music suitable for waltzing to is playing.*

NASSER: What a beautiful thing they've done with it! Isn't it? Oh, God and with music too!

RACHEL: It's like an incredible ship. I had no idea.

NASSER: He's a marvellous bloody boy, Rachel, I tell you.

RACHEL: You don't have to tell me.

NASSER: But I tell you everything five times.

RACHEL: At least.

NASSER: Am I a bad man to you then?

84

RACHEL: You are sometimes . . . careless.
NASSER: (*Moved*) Yes.
RACHEL: Dance with me. (*He goes to her.*) But we are learning.
NASSER: Where are those two buggers?

85. INT. BACK ROOM OF LAUNDRETTE. DAY.

OMAR *and* JOHNNY *are holding each other.*
JOHNNY: Nothing I can say, to make it up to you. There's only
    things I can do to show that I am . . . with you.
    (OMAR *starts to unbutton* JOHNNY's *shirt.*)

86. INT. LAUNDRETTE. DAY.

NASSER *and* RACHEL *are waltzing across the laundrette. Outside,
the old ladies are shifting about impatiently.*
NASSER: Of course, Johnny did all the physical work on this.
RACHEL: You're fond of him.
NASSER: I wish I could do something more to help the other
    deadbeat children like him. They hang about the road like
    pigeons, making a mess, doing nothing.
RACHEL: And you're tired of work.
NASSER: It's time I became a holy man.
RACHEL: A sadhu of South London.
NASSER: (*Surprised at her knowledge*) Yes. But first I must marry
    Omar off.

87. INT. BACK ROOM OF LAUNDRETTE. DAY.

OMAR *and* JOHNNY *are making love vigorously, enjoying themselves
thoroughly. Suddenly* OMAR *stops a moment, looks up, sees* NASSER
and RACHEL *waltzing across the laundrette.* OMAR *jumps up.*

88. INT. LAUNDRETTE. DAY.

NASSER *strides impatiently towards the door of the back room.*

89. INT. BACK ROOM OF LAUNDRETTE. DAY.

OMAR *and* JOHNNY *are quickly getting dressed.* NASSER *bursts into
the room.*
NASSER: What the hell are you doing? Sunbathing?

85

OMAR: Asleep, Uncle. We were shagged out. Where's Papa?

(NASSER *just looks at* OMAR. RACHEL *appears at the door behind him.*)

90.   INT. LAUNDRETTE. DAY.

The laundrette is open now. The ladies and other locals are doing their washing. The machines are whirring, sheets are being folded, magazines read, music played, video games played, etc.

   SALIM *arrives with* ZAKI. *They talk as they come in.*

ZAKI: Laundrettes are impossible. I've got two laundrettes and two ulcers. Plus . . . piles!

(GENGHIS, MOOSE *and the rest of the gang arrive.* MOOSE *goes into the laundrette, followed by* GENGHIS. GENGHIS *turns and forbids the rest of the* GANG *from entering. They wait restlessly outside.*

   JOHNNY *is talking to* RACHEL.)

RACHEL: What's your surname?

JOHNNY: Burfoot.

RACHEL: That's it. I know your mother.

(*The* TELEPHONE CHARACTER *is on the phone, talking eagerly to his Angela.*

   Through the window, OMAR, *who is talking to* NASSER, *sees* TANIA. *She is crossing the road and carrying a bouquet of flowers.*)

OMAR: I thought Papa just might make it today, Uncle.

NASSER: He said he never visits laundrettes.

(TANIA *comes in through the door.*)

JOHNNY: (*To* RACHEL) Oh good, it's Tania.

RACHEL: I've never met her. But she has a beautiful face.

(JOHNNY *leaves* RACHEL *and goes to* TANIA, *kissing her. He takes the flowers delightedly.*

   NASSER *is disturbed by the sudden unexpected appearance of his daughter, since he is with his mistress,* RACHEL.)

NASSER: (*To* OMAR) Who invited Tania, dammit?

(GENGHIS *and* MOOSE *shout out as they play the video game.*)

OMAR: I did, Uncle.

(*They watch as* TANIA *goes to* RACHEL *with* JOHNNY. JOHNNY *has no choice but to introduce* TANIA *and* RACHEL.)

86

TANIA: (*Smiles at* RACHEL) At last. After so many years in my family's life.

RACHEL: Tania, I do feel I know you.

TANIA: But you don't.

NASSER: (*Watching this*) Bring Tania over here.

TANIA: (*To* RACHEL) I don't mind my father having a mistress.

RACHEL: Good. I am so grateful.

NASSER: (*To* OMAR) Then marry her. (OMAR *looks at him.*) What's wrong with her? If I say marry her then you damn well do it!

TANIA: (*To* RACHEL) I don't mind my father spending our money on you.

RACHEL: Why don't you mind?

NASSER: (*To* OMAR) Start being nice to Tania. Take the pressure off my fucking head.

TANIA: (*To* RACHEL) Or my father being with you instead of with our mother.

NASSER: (*To* OMAR) Your penis works, doesn't it?

TANIA: (*To* RACHEL) But I don't like women who live off men.

NASSER: (*Shoving* OMAR *forward*) Get going then!

TANIA: (*To* RACHEL) That's a pretty disgusting parasitical thing, isn't it?

OMAR: (*To* TANIA) Tania, come and look at the spin-driers. They are rather interesting.

RACHEL: But tell me, who do you live off? And you must understand, we are of different generations, and different classes. Everything is waiting for you. The only thing that has ever waited for me is your father.

(*Then, with great dignity,* NASSER *goes to* RACHEL.)

NASSER: We'd better get going. See you boys.

(*He shakes hands warmly with* OMAR *and* JOHNNY. *And goes out with* RACHEL, *ignoring* TANIA.

Outside in the street, RACHEL *and* NASSER *begin to argue bitterly. They are watched by the rest of the* GANG. RACHEL *and* NASSER *finally walk away from each other, in different directions, sadly.*)

91. INT. LAUNDRETTE. DAY.

*The laundrette is full now, mostly with real punters doing their
washing and enjoying being there.*

GENGHIS *and* MOOSE *are still drinking.* GENGHIS *talks across
the laundrette to* JOHNNY. JOHNNY *is doing a service wash, folding
clothes.*

OMAR *is saying goodbye to* TANIA *at the door.*

SALIM *has hung back and is waiting for* OMAR, ZAKI *says
goodbye to him and goes, tentatively past the volatile breast-baring*
TANIA.

TANIA: (*To* OMAR) I want to leave home. I need to break away.
    You'll have to help me financially.
    (OMAR *nods enthusiastically.*)

GENGHIS: (*To* JOHNNY) Why don't you come out with us no
    more?

OMAR: (*To* TANIA) I'm drunk.

JOHNNY: (*To* GENGHIS) I'm busy here full-time, Genghis.

OMAR: (*To* TANIA) Will you marry me, Tania?

TANIA: (*To* OMAR) If you can get me some money.

GENGHIS: (*To* JOHNNY) Don't the Paki give you time off?

MOOSE: (*To* JOHNNY) I bet you ain't got the guts to ask him for
    time off.

SALIM: (*To* JOHNNY, *indicating* OMAR) Omo's getting married.
    (TANIA *goes.* SALIM *goes to* OMAR. *He puts his arm round him
    and takes him outside.* OMAR *is reluctant to go at first, but*
    SALIM *is firm and strong and pulls him out.* JOHNNY *watches.*)

GENGHIS: (*To* JOHNNY) You out with us tonight then?

92. EXT. STREET OUTSIDE LAUNDRETTE. DAY.

It is starting to get dark. OMAR *and* SALIM *stand beside Salim's
smart car.*

Eager and curious customers are still arriving. SALIM *nods
approvingly at them.*

Above them the huge pink flashing neon sign saying
'*POWDERS*'.

*Some kids are playing football in the street opposite the
laundrette.*

JOHNNY *rushes to the door of the laundrette. He shouts at the kids.*

JOHNNY: You mind these windows!
   (SALIM, *being watched by* JOHNNY, *starts to lead* OMAR *up
   the street, away from the laundrette.*)
SALIM: (*To* OMAR) I'm afraid you owe me a lot of money. The
   beard? Remember? Eh? Good. It's all coming back. I think
   I'd better have that money back, don't you?
OMAR: I haven't got money like that now.
SALIM: Because it's all in the laundrette?
   (GENGHIS *and* MOOSE *have come out of the laundrette and
   walked up the street away from it, parallel with* OMAR *and*
   SALIM. GENGHIS *stares contemptuously at* SALIM *and* MOOSE
   spits on the pavement. SALIM *ignores them.*)
   I'd better have a decent down payment then, of about half.
   (OMAR *nods.*) By the time Nasser has his annual party, say.
   Or I'll instruct him to get rid of the laundrette. You see, if
   anyone does anything wrong with me, I always destroy
   them.
   (JOHNNY *comes out of the laundrette and runs up behind*
   GENGHIS *and* MOOSE, *jumping on* MOOSE's *back. They turn
   the corner, away from* SALIM *and* OMAR. OMAR *watches them
   go anxiously, not understanding what* JOHNNY *could be doing
   with them.*)
OMAR: Took you a while to get on to us.
SALIM: Wanted to see what you'd do. How's your Papa? (OMAR
   shrugs.) So many books written and read. Politicians sought
   him out. Bhutto was his close friend. But we're nothing in
   England without money.

93.   INT. BETTING SHOP. DAY.
*There are only five or six people in the betting shop, all of them men.
   And the men are mostly old, in slippers and filthy suits; with
bandaged legs and stained shirts and unshaven milk-bottle-white
faces and National Health glasses.* NASSER *looks confident and
powerful beside them. He knows them. There's a good sense of
camaraderie amongst them.*
   When OMAR *goes into the betting shop* NASSER *is sitting on a
stool, a pile of betting slips in front of him, staring at one of the*

89

newspaper pages pinned to the wall. An OLD MAN is sitting next to NASSER, giving him advice.

OMAR goes to NASSER.

OMAR: (*Anxiously*) Uncle. (NASSER *ignores him.*) Uncle.

NASSER: (*Scribbling on betting slip*) Even royalty can't reach me in the afternoons.

OMAR: I've got to talk. About Salim.

NASSER: Is he squeezing your balls?

OMAR: Yes. I want your help, Uncle.

NASSER: (*Getting up*) You do it all now. It's up to you, boy.

(NASSER *goes to the betting counter and hands over his betting slips. He also hands over a thick pile of money.*

Over the shop PA we can hear that the race is beginning. It starts.

NASSER *listens as if hypnotized, staring wildly at the others in the shop, for sympathy, clenching his fists, stamping his feet and shouting loudly as his horse, 'Elvis', is among the front runners.*

OMAR *has never seen* NASSER *like this before.*)

(*To horse*) Come on, Elvis, my son. (*To* OMAR.) You'll just have to run the whole family yourself now. (*To horse.*) Go on, boy! (*To* OMAR.) You take control. (*To horse and others in shop.*) Yes, yes, yes, he's going to take it, the little bastard black beauty! (*To* OMAR.) It's all yours. Salim too. (*To horse.*) Do it, do it, do it, baby! No, no, no, no.

(NASSER *is rigid with self-loathing and disappointment as 'Elvis' loses the race. The betting slip falls from his hand. And he hangs his head in despair.*)

OMAR: Where's Rachel?

NASSER: You can't talk to her. She's busy pulling her hair out. If only your damn father were sober. I'd talk to him about her. He's the only one who knows anything. (*Facetious.*) I'd ask him about Salim if I were you.

(OMAR *stares at* NASSER *in fury and disgust. He storms out of the betting shop, just as the next race – a dog race – is about to start.*)

94. INT. LAUNDRETTE. EVENING.
The laundrette is fully functional now, busy and packed with customers.

Music is playing – a soprano aria from Madame
Butterfly.

*Customers are reading magazines. They are talking, watching
TV with the sound turned down and one white man is singing along
with the Puccini which he knows word for word.*

The TELEPHONE CHARACTER *is yelling into the bright new
yellow phone.*

TELEPHONE CHARACTER: (*Into phone*) 'Course I'll look after it!
    I'll come round every other night. At least. Honest. I want
    children!

    (OMAR *walks around the laundrette, watching over it, proud
    and stern. He helps people if the doors of the renovated
    machines are stiff.*

    *And he hands people baskets to move their washing about in.
    Shots of people putting money into the machines.*

    But JOHNNY *isn't there.* OMAR *doesn't know where he is and
    looks outside anxiously for him. He is worried and upset about
    Salim's demand for money.*

    Finally OMAR *goes out into the street and asks a kid if he's
    seen* JOHNNY.)

95.   INT. TOP HALL OF THE HOUSE JOHNNY'S MOVED INTO.
NIGHT.
*A party is going on in one of the rooms on this floor. The noise is
tremendous and people are falling about the hall.*

   A PAKISTANI STUDENT, *a man in his late twenties with an
intelligent face, is bent over someone who has collapsed across the
doorway between room and hall.*

PAKISTANI STUDENT: (*As* OMAR *goes past*) There's only one
    word for your uncle. (OMAR *walks on fastidiously, ignoring
    them, to Johnny's door. The* STUDENT *yells.*) Collaborator
    with the white man!

    (OMAR *knocks on Johnny's door.*)

96.   INT. JOHNNY'S ROOM. NIGHT.
OMAR *goes into Johnny's room.* JOHNNY *is lying on the bed,
drinking, wearing only a pair of boxer shorts.*

   OMAR *stands at the open door.*

JOHNNY *runs to the door and screams up the hall to the* PAKISTANI STUDENT.

JOHNNY: Didn't I tell you, didn't I tell you 'bout that noise last night? (*Pause.*) Well, didn't I?

(*The* PAKISTANI STUDENT *stares contemptuously at him. The drunks lie where they are.* JOHNNY *slams the door of his room. And* OMAR *starts on him.*)

OMAR: Where did you go? You just disappeared!

JOHNNY: Drinking, I went. With me old mates. It's not illegal.

OMAR: 'Course it is. Laundrettes are a big commitment. Why aren't you at work?

JOHNNY: It'll be closing time soon. You'll be locking the place up, and coming to bed.

OMAR: No, it never closes. And one of us has got to be there. That way we begin to make money.

JOHNNY: You're getting greedy.

OMAR: I want big money. I'm not gonna be beat down by this country. When we were at school, you and your lot kicked me all round the place. And what are you doing now? Washing my floor. That's how I like it. Now get to work. Get to work I said. Or you're fired!

(OMAR *grabs him and pulls him up.* JOHNNY *doesn't resist.* OMAR *throws his shirt and shoes at him.* JOHNNY *dresses.*)

JOHNNY: (*Touching him*) What about you?

OMAR: I don't wanna see you for a little while. I got some big thinking to do.

(JOHNNY *looks regretfully at him.*)

JOHNNY: But today, it's been the best day!

OMAR: Yeah. Almost the best day.

97.   INT. TOP HALL. NIGHT.

JOHNNY, *dressed now, walks past the party room. The* PAKISTANI STUDENT *is now playing a tabla in the hall.* JOHNNY *ignores him, though the* STUDENT *looks ironically at him.*

98.   INT. BOTTOM ENTRANCE HALL OF THE HOUSE. NIGHT.

JOHNNY *stops by a wall box in the hall. He pulls a bunch of keys*

out of his pocket and unlocks the wall box.
  He reaches in and pulls a switch.

99. EXT. OUTSIDE THE HOUSE. NIGHT.
JOHNNY *walks away from the house. He has plunged the party
room into darkness. In the room people are screaming.*
  The PAKISTANI STUDENT *yells out of the window at* JOHNNY.
PAKISTANI STUDENT: You are not human! You are cold
    people, you English, the big icebergs of Europe!
    (OMAR *stands at the next window along, looking out. This
    room is lighted.*
      JOHNNY *chuckles to himself as he walks jauntily away.*)

100. INT. LAUNDRETTE. NIGHT.
Nina Simone's smooth 'Walk On By' playing in the laundrette.
  And there are still plenty of people around.
  The TELEPHONE CHARACTER *has turned to the wall, head
down, to concentrate on his conversation.*
  A MAN *is asleep on a bench.* JOHNNY *walks past him, notices
he's asleep and suddenly pokes him. The* MAN *jumps awake.*
JOHNNY *points at the man's washing.*
  A young black COUPLE *are dancing, holding each other sleepily
as they wait for their washing.*
  A BUM *comes in through the door, slowly, with difficulty in
walking. He's wearing a large black overcoat with the collar turned
up.* JOHNNY *watches him.*
JOHNNY: Hey!
    (*The* BUM *doesn't respond.* JOHNNY *goes to him and takes
    his arm, about to chuck him out. Then the* BUM *turns to*
    JOHNNY.)
PAPA: I recognize you at least. Let me sit.
    (JOHNNY *leads* PAPA *up the laundrette.*
      The TELEPHONE CHARACTER *throws down the receiver
    and walks out.*)
JOHNNY: (*Deferential now*) We were expecting you today.
PAPA: I've come.
JOHNNY: The invitation was for two o'clock, Mr Ali.
PAPA: (*Looking at his watch*) It's only ten past now. I thought I'd

come to the wrong place. That I was suddenly in a ladies'
hairdressing salon in Pinner, where one might get a pink
rinse. Do you do a pink rinse, Johnny? Or are you still a
fascist?

JOHNNY: You used to give me a lot of good advice, sir. When I
was little.

PAPA: When you were little. What's it made of you? Are you a
politician? Journalist? A trade unionist? No, you are an
underpants cleaner. (*Self-mocking.*) Oh dear, the working
class are such a great disappointment to me.

JOHNNY: I haven't made much of myself.

PAPA: You'd better get on and do something.

JOHNNY: Yes. Here, we can do something.

PAPA: Help me. I want my son out of this underpants cleaning
condition. I want him reading in college. You tell him: you
go to college. He must have knowledge. We all must, now.
In order to see clearly what's being done and to whom in
this country. Right?

JOHNNY: I don't know. It depends on what he wants.

PAPA: No. (*Strongly.*) You must use your influence. (PAPA *gets
up and walks out slowly.* JOHNNY *watches him go, sadly.*
PAPA *turns.*) Not a bad dump you got here.

101. EXT. OUTSIDE THE LAUNDRETTE. NIGHT.
PAPA *walks away from the laundrette.*

102. EXT. THE DRIVE OF NASSER'S HOUSE. DAY.
JOHNNY *has come by bus to Nasser's house. And* OMAR *opens the
front door to him.* JOHNNY *is about to step into the house.* OMAR
takes him out into the drive.

JOHNNY: What you make me come all this way for?

OMAR: Gotta talk.

JOHNNY: You bloody arse. (*At the side of the house a strange
sight.* TANIA *is climbing a tree.* BILQUIS *is at the bottom of the
tree yelling instructions to her in Urdu.* JOHNNY *and* OMAR
watch.) What's going on?

OMAR: It's heavy, man. Bilquis is making magical potions from
leaves and bird beaks and stuff. She's putting them on Rachel.

94

(JOHNNY *watches* TANIA *groping for leaves in amazement.*)

JOHNNY: Is it working?

OMAR: Rachel rang me. She's got the vicar round. He's
performing an exorcism right now. The furniture's shaking.
Her trousers are walking by themselves.

103. INT. NASSER'S ROOM. DAY.

OMAR *and* JOHNNY *and* NASSER *are sitting at a table in Nasser's
room, playing cards.* NASSER *is sulky. He puts his cards down.*

NASSER: I'm out.

  (*He gets up and goes and lies down on the bed, his arm over his
  face.*

    OMAR *and* JOHNNY *continue playing. They put their cards
    down.* JOHNNY *wins. He collects the money.*)

OMAR: Salim's gotta have money. Soon. A lot of money. He
threatened me. (*They get up and walk out of the room, talking
in low voices.* NASSER *lies there on the bed, not listening but
brooding.*) I didn't wanna tell you before. I thought I could
raise the money on the profits from the laundrette. But it's
impossible in the time.

104. INT. HALL OUTSIDE NASSER'S ROOM. DAY.

They walk down the hall to the verandah.

JOHNNY: This city's chock-full of money. When I used to want
money –

OMAR: You'd steal it.

JOHNNY: Yeah. Decide now if you want it to be like that again.

105. INT. VERANDAH. DAY.

They reach the verandah. Outside, in the garden, the two younger
DAUGHTERS *are playing.*

  At the other end of the verandah BILQUIS *and* TANIA *are sitting
on the sofa, a table in front of them.* BILQUIS *is mixing various
ingredients in a big bowl – vegetables, bits of bird, leaves, some dog
urine, the squeezed eyeball of a newt, half a goldfish, etc. We see her
slicing the goldfish.*

  At the same time she is dictating a letter to TANIA, *which* TANIA
takes down on a blue airletter. TANIA *looks pretty fed-up.*

95

OMAR *and* JOHNNY *sit down and watch them.*

OMAR: She's illiterate. Tania's writing to her sister for her. Bilquis is thinking of going back, after she's hospitalized Rachel. (BILQUIS *looks up at them, her eyes dark and her face humourless.*) Nasser's embarked on a marathon sulk. He's going for the world record.
(*Pause.* JOHNNY *changes the subject back when* TANIA – *suspecting them of laughing at her – gives them a sharp look.*)

JOHNNY: We'll just have to do a job to get the money.

OMAR: I don't want you going back to all that.

JOHNNY: Just to get us through, Omo. It's for both of us. If we're going to go on. You want that, don't you?

OMAR: Yes. I want you.
(*Suddenly* NASSER *appears at the door and starts abusing* BILQUIS *in loud Urdu, telling her that the magic business is stupid, etc. But* BILQUIS *has a rougher, louder tongue. She says, among other things, in Urdu, that* NASSER *is a big fat black man who should get out of her sight for ever.*
TANIA *is very distressed by this, hands over face. Suddenly she gets up. The magic potion bowl is knocked over, the evil ingredients spilling over Bilquis' feet.* BILQUIS *screams.*
JOHNNY *starts laughing.* BILQUIS *picks up the rest of the bowl and throws the remainder of the potion over* NASSER.)

106. EXT. OUTSIDE A SMART HOUSE. NIGHT.
A semi-detached house. A hedge around the front of the house.
JOHNNY *is forcing the front window. He knows what he's doing. He climbs in. He indicates to* OMAR *that he should follow. And* OMAR *follows.*

107. INT. FRONT ROOM OF THE HOUSE. NIGHT.
They're removing the video and TV and going out the front door with them. Their car is parked outside.
Suddenly a tiny KID *of about eight is standing behind them at the bottom of the stairs. He is an* INDIAN KID. OMAR *looks at him, the* KID *opens his mouth to yell.* OMAR *grabs the* KID *and slams his hand over his mouth. While he holds the* KID, JOHNNY *goes out with the stereo. Then the compact disc player.*

OMAR *leaves the stunned* KID *and makes a run for it.*

108. INT. BACK ROOM OF LAUNDRETTE. NIGHT.
*There are televisions, stereos, radios, videos, etc. stacked up in the
back room.* OMAR *stands there looking at them.*

    JOHNNY *comes in struggling with a video.* OMAR *smiles at him.*
JOHNNY *doesn't respond.*

109. INT. HALL. DAY.
The top hall of the house JOHNNY *lives in.* JOHNNY, *wearing jeans
and T-shirt, barefoot, only recently having woken up, is banging on
the door of the Pakistani student's room.*

    OMAR *is standing beside him, smartly dressed and carrying a
briefcase. He's spent the night with* JOHNNY. *And now he's going to
the laundrette.*
JOHNNY: (*To door*) Rent day! Rent up, man!
    (OMAR *watches him.* JOHNNY *looks unhappy.*)
OMAR: I said it would bring you down, stealing again. It's no
    good for you. You need a brand new life.
    (*The* PAKISTANI STUDENT *opens the door.* OMAR *moves
    away. To* JOHNNY.) Party tonight. Then we'll be in the
    clear.
PAKISTANI STUDENT: Unblock the toilet, yes, Johnny?
JOHNNY: (*Looking into the room*) Tonight. You're not doing
    nothing political in there, are you, man? I've gotta take a
    look.
    (OMAR, *laughing, moves away.* JOHNNY *shoves the door hard
    and the* PAKISTANI STUDENT *relents.*)

110. INT. PAKISTANI STUDENT'S ROOM. DAY.
JOHNNY *goes into the room. A young* PAKISTANI WOMAN *is sitting
on the bed with a* CHILD.

    A younger PAKISTANI BOY *of about fourteen is standing behind
her. And across the room a* PAKISTANI GIRL *of seventeen.*
PAKISTANI STUDENT: My family, escaping persecution.
    (JOHNNY *looks at him.*) Are you a good man or are you a
    bad man?

111. EXT. COUNTRY LANE AND DRIVE OF NASSER'S HOUSE.
EVENING.

OMAR *and* JOHNNY *are sitting in the back of a mini-cab.*

JOHNNY *is as dressed up as is* OMAR, *but in fashionable street clothes rather than an expensive dark suit.* JOHNNY *will be out of keeping sartorially with the rest of the party.*

The young ASIAN DRIVER *moves the car towards Nasser's house.*

The house is a blaze of light and noise. And the drive is full of cars and PAKISTANIS *and* INDIANS *getting noisily out of them. Looking at the house, the lights, the extravagance,* JOHNNY *laughs sarcastically.*

OMAR, *paying the driver, looks irritably at* JOHNNY.

JOHNNY: What does he reckon he is, your uncle? Some kinda big Gatsby geezer? (OMAR *gives him a cutting look.*) Maybe this just isn't my world. You're right. Still getting married?
(*They both get out of the car.* OMAR *walks towards the house.*
JOHNNY *stands there a moment, not wanting to face it all.*

When OMAR *has almost reached the front door and* TANIA *has come out to hug him,* JOHNNY *moves towards the house.*

TANIA *hugs* JOHNNY.

OMAR *looks into the house and sees* SALIM *and* CHERRY *in the crowd in the front room. He waves at* SALIM *but* SALIM *ignores him.* CHERRY *is starting to look pregnant.*

BILQUIS *is standing at the end of the hall. She greets* OMAR *in Urdu. And he replies in rudimentary Urdu.*

JOHNNY *feels rather odd since he's the only white person in sight.*)

112. INT/EXT. THE VERANDAH, PATIO AND GARDEN.
EVENING.

The house, patio and garden are full of well-off, well-dressed, well-pissed, middle-class PAKISTANIS *and* INDIANS.

The American, DICK, *and the* ENGLISHMAN *are talking together.*

DICK: England needs more young men like Omar and Johnny, from what I can see.

ENGLISHMAN: (*Slightly camp*) The more boys like that the better.
(*We see* OMAR *on the verandah talking confidently to various people. Occasionally he glances at* SALIM *who is engrossed in*

conversation with ZAKI *and Zaki's* WIFE. *A snatch of their conversation.*)

SALIM: Now Cherry is pregnant I will be buying a house. I am going to have many children . . .

(BILQUIS *is there. She is alone but there is a fierceness and cheerfulness about her that we haven't noticed before.*

JOHNNY *doesn't know who to talk to.* CHERRY *goes up to him.*)

CHERRY: Please, can you take charge of the music for us?

(JOHNNY *looks at her. Then he shakes his head.*

NASSER, *in drunken, ebullient mood, takes* OMAR *across the room to* ZAKI, *who is with* SALIM.)

ZAKI: (*Shaking hands with* OMAR) Omar, my boy.

(SALIM *moves away.*)

NASSER: (*To* OMAR, *of* ZAKI) Help him. (*To* ZAKI.) Now tell him, please.

ZAKI: Oh God, Omo, I've got these two damn laundrettes in your area. I need big advice on them.

(*We hear Omar's voice as we look at the party.*)

OMAR: I won't advise you. If the laundrettes are a trouble to you I'll pay you rent for them plus a percentage of the profits.

NASSER: How about it, Zaki? He'll run them with Johnny.

(*We see* TANIA *talking to two interested* PAKISTANI MEN *in their middle twenties who see her as marriageable and laugh at everything she says. But* TANIA *is looking at* JOHNNY *who is on his own, drinking. He also dances, bending his knees and doing an inconspicuous handjive. He smiles at* TANIA.

TANIA *goes across to* JOHNNY. *He whispers something in her ear. She leads* JOHNNY *by the hand out into the garden.*

BILQUIS *looks in fury at* NASSER, *blaming him for this. He turns away from her.*

ZAKI *is happily explaining to his wife about the deal with* OMAR.)

113.   EXT. GARDEN. EVENING.

TANIA *leads* JOHNNY *across the garden, towards the little garden house at the end. A bicycle is leaning against it. She takes off her shoes. And they hold each other and dance.*

99

114. INT. THE HOUSE. EVENING.

SALIM *is on his own a moment.* OMAR *moves towards him.* SALIM *walks out and across the garden.*

115. EXT. GARDEN. EVENING.

OMAR *follows* SALIM *across the lawn.*

OMAR: I've got it. (SALIM *turns to him.*) The instalment. It's hefty, Salim. More than you wanted.

(OMAR *fumbles for the money in his jacket pocket. At the end of the garden* JOHNNY *and* TANIA *are playing around with a bicycle.* OMAR, *shaking, drops some of the money.* SALIM *raises his hand in smiling rejection.*)

SALIM: Don't ever offer me money. It was an educational test I put on you. To make you see you did a wrong thing.

(TANIA *and* JOHNNY *are now riding the bicycle on the lawn.*) Don't in future bite the family hand when you can eat out of it. If you need money just ask me. Years ago your uncles lifted me up. And I will do the same for you.

(*Through this* OMAR *has become increasingly concerned as* TANIA, *with* JOHNNY *on the back of the bicycle, is riding at* Salim's *back.* OMAR *shouts out.*)

OMAR: Tania!

(*And he tries to pull* SALIM *out of the way. But* TANIA *crashes into* SALIM, *knocking him flying flat on his face.* NASSER *comes rushing down the lawn.*

TANIA *and* JOHNNY *lie laughing on their backs.*

SALIM *gets up quickly, furiously, and goes to punch* JOHNNY. OMAR *and* NASSER *grab an arm of* SALIM's *each.* JOHNNY *laughs in* SALIM's *face.*)

(*To* SALIM) All right, all right, he's no one.

(SALIM *calms down quickly and just raises a warning finger at* JOHNNY. *The confrontation is mainly diverted by* NASSER *going for* TANIA.)

NASSER: (*To* TANIA) You little bitch! (*He grabs at* TANIA *to hit her.* JOHNNY *pulls her away.*) What the hell d'you think you're doing?

SALIM: (*To* NASSER) Can't you control your bloody people?

(*And he abuses* NASSER *in Urdu.* NASSER *curses and scowls* in English:) Why should you be able to? You've gambled most of your money down the toilet! (SALIM *turns and walks away.*)

TANIA: (*Pointing after him*) That smooth suppository owns us! Everything! Our education, your businesses, Rachel's stockings. It's his!

NASSER: (*To* OMAR) Aren't you two getting married?

OMAR: Yes, yes, any day now.

TANIA: I'd rather drink my own urine.

OMAR: I hear it can be quite tasty, with a slice of lemon.

NASSER: Get out of my sight, Tania!

TANIA: I'm going further than that.

(NASSER *turns and storms away. As he walks up the lawn we see that* BILQUIS *has been standing a quarter of the way down the lawn, witnessing all this.*

NASSER *stops for a moment beside her, not looking at her. He walks on.*)

OMAR: (*To* JOHNNY) Let's get out of here.

TANIA: (*To* JOHNNY) Take me.

(OMAR *shakes his head and takes* JOHNNY'*s hand.*)

OMAR: Salim'll give us a lift.

JOHNNY: What?

OMAR: I need him for something I've got in mind.

116. INT. SALIM'S CAR. NIGHT.

SALIM *is driving* JOHNNY *and* OMAR *along a country lane, fast, away from Nasser's house.*

JOHNNY *is sitting in the back, looking out of the window.*

OMAR *is sarcastic for* JOHNNY'*s unheeding benefit and undetected by the humourless* SALIM.

OMAR: Well, thanks, Salim, you know. For saving the laundrette and everything. And for giving us a lift. Our car's bust.

SALIM: (*Accelerating*) Got to get to a little liaison. (*To* JOHNNY.) He doesn't have to thank me. Eh, Johnny? What's your problem with me, Johnny?

JOHNNY: (*Eventually, and tough*) Salim, we know what you sell, man. Know the kids you sell it to. It's shit, man. Shit.

SALIM: Haven't you noticed? People are shit. I give them what they want. I don't criticize. I supply. The laws of business apply.

JOHNNY: Christ, what a view of people. Eh, Omo? You think that's a filthy shit thing, don't you, Omo?

(*Suddenly* SALIM *steps on the brakes. They skid to a stop on the edge of a steep drop away from the road.*)

SALIM: Get out!

(JOHNNY *opens the car door. He looks down the steep hill and across the windy Kent landscape. He leans back in his seat, closing the car door.*)

JOHNNY: I don't like the country. The snakes make me nervous.

(SALIM *laughs and drives off.*)

117.   INT. SALIM'S CAR. NIGHT.

They've reached South London, near the laundrette.

   OMAR'S *been explaining to* SALIM *about his new scheme.*

OMAR: . . . So I was talking to Zaki about it. I want to take over his two laundrettes. He's got no idea.

SALIM: None.

OMAR: Do them up. With this money. (*He pats his pocket.*)

SALIM: Yeah. Is it enough?

OMAR: I thought maybe you could come in with me . . . financially.

SALIM: Yeah. I'm looking for some straight outlets. (*Pause.*) You're a smart bastard. (*Suddenly.*) Hey, hey, hey . . .

(*And he sees, in the semi-darkness near the football ground, a group of roaming laughing* LADS. *They are walking into a narrow lane.* SALIM *slows the car down and enters the street behind them, following them now, watching them and explaining. To* JOHNNY.) These people. What a waste of life. They're filthy and ignorant. They're just nothing. But they abuse people. (*To* OMAR.) Our people. (*To* JOHNNY.) All over England, Asians, as you call us, are beaten, burnt to death. Always we are intimidated. What these scum need – (*and he slams the car into gear and starts to drive forward fast*) – is a taste of their own piss.

(*He accelerates fast, and mounting the pavement, drives at the* LADS *ahead of him.* MOOSE *turns and sees the car. They scatter and run. Another of the* LADS *is* GENGHIS. *Some of the others we will recognize as mates of his.*

GENGHIS *gets in close against a wall, picking up a lump of wood to smash through the car windscreen. But he doesn't have time to fling it and drops it as* SALIM *drives at him, turning away at the last minute.* GENGHIS *sees clearly who is in the front of the car.*

As SALIM *turns the car away from* GENGHIS, MOOSE *is suddenly standing stranded in the centre of the road.* SALIM *can't avoid him.* MOOSE *jumps aside but* SALIM *drives over his foot.* MOOSE *screams.*

SALIM *drives on.*)

118.   INT. JOHNNY'S ROOM. NIGHT.
OMAR *and* JOHNNY *have made love.* OMAR *appears to be asleep, lying across the bed.*

JOHNNY *gets up, walks across the room and picks up a bottle of whisky. He drinks.*

119.   INT. ANOTHER LAUNDRETTE. DAY.
This is a much smaller and less splendid laundrette than Omar's.

OMAR *is looking it over 'expertly'.* ZAKI *is awaiting Omar's verdict. This is Zaki's problem laundrette.*

SALIM *is also there, striding moodily about.*
OMAR: I think I can do something with this. Me and my
      partner.
ZAKI: Take it. I trust you and your family.
OMAR: Salim?
SALIM: I'd happily put money into it.
OMAR: All right. Wait a minute.

120.   EXT. OUTSIDE THIS SMALLER LAUNDRETTE. DAY.
JOHNNY *is morosely sitting in the car, examining himself in the car mirror. In the mirror, at the far end of the street, he sees a figure on crutches watching them. This is* MOOSE.

103

OMAR *comes out of the laundrette and talks to* JOHNNY *through the car window.*

OMAR: You wanna look at this place? Think we could do something with it?

JOHNNY: Can't tell without seeing it.

OMAR: Come on, then.

JOHNNY: Not if that scum Salim's there.

(OMAR *turns away angrily and walks back into the laundrette.*)

121. EXT. OUTSIDE OMAR AND JOHNNY'S BEAUTIFUL LAUNDRETTE. DAY.

GENGHIS *is standing on the roof of the laundrette, a plank of wood studded with nails in his hand.*

Across the street, in the alley and behind cars, the LADS *are waiting and watching the laundrette.* MOOSE *is with them, hobbling. Inside,* JOHNNY *washes the floor.* TANIA, *not seeing* GENGHIS *or the* LADS, *walks down the street towards the laundrette.*

122. INT. LAUNDRETTE. DAY.

JOHNNY *is washing the floor of the laundrette. A white* MAN *opens a washing machine and starts picking prawns out of it, putting them in a black plastic bag.* JOHNNY *watches in amazement.*

TANIA *comes into the laundrette to say goodbye to* JOHNNY. *She is carrying a bag.*

TANIA: (*Excited*) I'm going.

JOHNNY: Where?

TANIA: London. Away.

(*Some* KIDS *are playing football outside, dangerously near the laundrette windows.* JOHNNY *goes to the window and bangs on it. He spots a* LAD *and* MOOSE *watching the laundrette from across the street.* JOHNNY *waves at them. They ignore him.*)

(*To him*) I'm going, to live my life. You can come.

JOHNNY: No good jobs like this in London.

TANIA: Omo just runs you around everywhere like a servant.

JOHNNY: Well. I'll stay here with my friend and fight it out.

TANIA: My family, Salim and all, they'll swallow you up like a little kebab.

JOHNNY: I couldn't just leave him now. Don't ask me to. You

ever touched him? (*She shakes her head.*) I wouldn't trust
him, though.
TANIA: Better go. (*She kisses him and turns and goes. He stands at
the door and watches her go.*)

123. EXT. OUTSIDE THE LAUNDRETTE. DAY.
From the roof GENGHIS *watches* TANIA *walk away from the
laundrette.*
      At the end of the street, Salim's car turns the corner. A LAD
standing on the corner signals to GENGHIS. GENGHIS *nods at the*
LADS *in the alley opposite and holds his piece of wood ready.*

124. INT. CLUB/BAR. DAY.
NASSER *and* RACHEL *are sitting at a table in the club/bar. They
have been having an intense, terrible, sad conversation. Now they
are staring at each other.* NASSER *holds her hand. She withdraws
her hand.*
      TARIQ *comes over to the table with two drinks. He puts them
down. He wants to talk to* NASSER. NASSER *touches his arm,
without looking up. And* TARIQ *goes.*
RACHEL: So . . . so . . . so that's it.
NASSER: Why? Why d'you have to leave me now? (*She shrugs.*)
      After all these days.
RACHEL: Years.
NASSER: Why say you're taking from my family?
RACHEL: Their love and money. Yes, apparently I am.
NASSER: No.
RACHEL: And it's not possible to enjoy being so hated.
NASSER: It'll stop.
RACHEL: Her work. (*She pulls up her jumper to reveal her
      blotched, marked stomach. If possible we should suspect for a
      moment that she is pregnant.*) And I am being cruel to her. It
      is impossible.
NASSER: Let me kiss you. (*She gets up.*) Oh, Christ. (*She turns to
      go.*) Oh, love. Don't go. Don't, Rachel. Don't go.

125. EXT. OUTSIDE LAUNDRETTE. DAY.
SALIM *is sitting in his car outside the laundrette.* GENGHIS *stands*

above him on the roof, watching. Across the street the LADS *wait in the alley, alert.*

SALIM *gets out of his car.*

126.   EXT. OUTSIDE ANWAR'S CLUB. DAY.
RACHEL *walks away from the club.* NASSER *stands at the door and watches her go.*

127.   EXT. OUTSIDE PAPA'S HOUSE. DAY.
NASSER *gets out of his car and walks towards Papa's house. The door is broken and he pushes it, going into the hall, to the bottom of the stairs.*

128.   EXT. OUTSIDE THE LAUNDRETTE. DAY.
SALIM *walks into the laundrette.*

129.   INT. PAPA'S HOUSE. DAY.
NASSER *sadly climbs the filthy stairs of the house in which Papa's flat is.*

130.   INT. LAUNDRETTE. DAY.
SALIM *has come into the busy laundrette.* JOHNNY *is working.*
SALIM: I want to talk to Omo about business.
JOHNNY: I dunno where he is.
SALIM: Is it worth waiting?
JOHNNY: In my experience it's always worth waiting for Omo.
     (*The* TELEPHONE CHARACTER *is yelling into the receiver.*)
TELEPHONE CHARACTER: No, no, I promise I'll look after it. I
     want a child, don't I? Right, I'm coming round now! (*He
     slams the receiver down. Then he starts to dial again.*)

131.   INT. PAPA'S HOUSE. DAY.
NASSER *has reached the top of the stairs and the door to Papa's flat. He opens the door with his key. He walks along the hall to Papa's room. He stops at the open door to Papa's room.* PAPA *is lying in bed completely still.* NASSER *looks at him, worried.*

132. EXT. OUTSIDE THE LAUNDRETTE. DAY.
The LADS *are waiting in the alley opposite.* GENGHIS *gives them a signal from the roof.*

The LADS *run across the street and start to smash up Salim's car with big sticks, laying into the headlights, the windscreen, the roof, etc.*

133. INT. LAUNDRETTE. DAY.
We are looking at the TELEPHONE CHARACTER. *He is holding the receiver in one hand. His other hand over his mouth.* SALIM *sees him and then turns to see, out of the laundrette window, his car being demolished.*

134. INT. PAPA'S ROOM. DAY.
NASSER *walks into Papa's room.* PAPA *hears him and looks up.* PAPA *struggles to get to the edge of the bed, and thrusts himself into the air.*

NASSER *goes towards him and they embrace warmly, fervently. Then* NASSER *sits down on the bed next to his brother.*

135. EXT. OUTSIDE THE LAUNDRETTE. DAY.
SALIM *runs out of the laundrette towards his car. He grabs one of the* LADS *and smashes the* LAD's *head on the side of the car.*

GENGHIS *is standing above them, on the edge of the roof.*
GENGHIS: (*Yells*) Hey! Paki! Hey! Paki!

136. INT. PAPA'S ROOM. DAY.
PAPA *and* NASSER *sit side by side on the bed.*
PAPA: This damn country has done us in. That's why I am like this. We should be there. Home.
NASSER: But that country has been sodomized by religion. It is beginning to interfere with the making of money.
Compared with everywhere, it is a little heaven here.

137. EXT. OUTSIDE THE LAUNDRETTE. DAY.
SALIM *looks up at* GENGHIS *standing on the edge of the roof. Suddenly* GENGHIS *jumps down, on top of* SALIM, *pulling* SALIM *to the ground with him.*

GENGHIS *quickly gets to his feet. And as* SALIM *gets up,* GENGHIS *hits him across the face with the studded piece of wood, tearing* SALIM'S *face.*

JOHNNY *is watching from inside the laundrette.*

138.   INT. PAPA'S ROOM. DAY.

PAPA *and* NASSER *are sitting on the bed.*

PAPA: Why are you unhappy?

NASSER: Rachel has left me. I don't know what I'm going to do.
   (*He gets up and goes to the door of the balcony.*)

139.   EXT. OUTSIDE THE LAUNDRETTE. DAY.

SALIM, *streaming blood, rushes at* GENGHIS. GENGHIS *smashes him in the stomach with the piece of wood.*

140.   EXT. SOUTH LONDON STREET. DAY.

OMAR *and* ZAKI *are walking along a South London street, away from Zaki's small laundrette.*

   Across the street is the club/bar. TARIQ *is just coming out. He waves at* OMAR.

ZAKI: So you're planning an armada of laundrettes?

OMAR: What do you think of the dry-cleaners?

ZAKI: They are the past. But then they are the present also.
   Mostly they are the past. But they are going to be the future too, don't you think?

141.   EXT. OUTSIDE THE LAUNDRETTE. DAY.

SALIM *is on the ground.* MOOSE *goes to him and whacks him with his crutch.* SALIM *lies still.* GENGHIS *kicks* SALIM *in the back. He is about to kick him again.*

   JOHNNY *is standing at the door of the laundrette. He moves towards* GENGHIS.

JOHNNY: He'll die.
   (GENGHIS *kicks* SALIM *again.* JOHNNY *loses his temper, rushes at* GENGHIS *and pushes him up against the car.*)
   I said: leave it out!
   (*One of the* LADS *moves towards* JOHNNY. GENGHIS *shakes his head at the* LAD. SALIM *starts to pull himself up off the*

floor. JOHNNY *holds* GENGHIS *like a lover. To* SALIM.)
Get out of here!
(GENGHIS *punches* JOHNNY *in the stomach.* GENGHIS *and*
      JOHNNY *start to fight.* GENGHIS *is strong but* JOHNNY *is
quick.* JOHNNY *tries twice to stop the fight, pulling away from*
GENGHIS.)
All right, let's leave it out now, eh?
(SALIM *crawls away.* GENGHIS *hits* JOHNNY *very hard and*
JOHNNY *goes down.*)

142.   EXT. STREET. DAY.
ZAKI *and* OMAR *turn the corner, into the street where the fight is
taking place.* ZAKI *sees* SALIM *staggering up the other side of the
street.* ZAKI *goes to him.*

   OMAR *runs towards the fight.* JOHNNY *is being badly beaten now.
A* LAD *grabs* OMAR. OMAR *struggles.*

   Suddenly the sound of police sirens. The fight scatters. As it does,
GENGHIS *throws his lump of wood through the laundrette window,
showering glass over the punters gathered round the window.*

   OMAR *goes to* JOHNNY, *who is barely conscious.*

143.   EXT. BALCONY OF PAPA'S FLAT. DAY.
NASSER *is standing leaning over the balcony, looking across the
railway track.* PAPA *comes through the balcony door and stands
behind him, in his pyjamas.*
NASSER: You still look after me, eh? But I'm finished.
PAPA: Only Omo matters.
NASSER: I'll make sure he's fixed up with a good business
   future.
PAPA: And marriage?
NASSER: I'm working on that.
PAPA: Tania is a possibility?
   (NASSER *nods confidently, perhaps over-confidently.*)

144.   INT. BACK ROOM OF LAUNDRETTE. DAY.
OMAR *is bathing* JOHNNY's *badly bashed up face at the sink in the
back room of the laundrette.*
OMAR: All right?

JOHNNY: What d'you mean all right? How can I be all right?
I'm in the state I'm in. (*Pause.*) I'll be handsome. But
where exactly am I?

OMAR: Where you should be. With me.

JOHNNY: No. Where does all this leave me?

OMAR: Are you crying?

JOHNNY: Where does it? Kiss me then.

OMAR: Don't cry. Your hand hurts too. That's why.

JOHNNY: Hey.

OMAR: What?

JOHNNY: I better go. I think I had, yeah.

OMAR: You were always going, at school. Always running
about, you. Your hand is bad. I couldn't pin you down
then.

JOHNNY: And now I'm going again. Give me my hand back.

OMAR: You're dirty. You're beautiful.

JOHNNY: I'm serious. Don't keep touching me.

OMAR: I'm going to give you a wash.

JOHNNY: You don't listen to anything.

OMAR: I'm filling this sink.

JOHNNY: Don't.

OMAR: Get over here! (OMAR *fills the sink.* JOHNNY *turns and
goes out of the room.*) Johnny.
(*We follow* JOHNNY *out through the laundrette.*)

145.   EXT. THE BALCONY. DAY.
PAPA *turns away from* NASSER.
   A train is approaching, rushing towards NASSER. *Suddenly it is
passing him and for a moment, if this is technically possible, he sees*
TANIA *sitting reading in the train, her bag beside her. He cries out,
but he is drowned out by the train.*
   *If it is not possible for him to see her, then we go into the train
with her and perhaps from her POV in the train look at the balcony,
the two figures, at the back view of the flat passing by.*

146.   INT. LAUNDRETTE. DAY.
JOHNNY *has got to the door of the laundrette.* OMAR *has rushed to*

110

the door of the back room.

The shattered glass from the window is still all over the floor. A cold wind blows through the half-lit laundrette.

JOHNNY stops at the door of the laundrette. He turns towards OMAR.

147. INT. BACK ROOM OF LAUNDRETTE. DAY.
As the film finishes, as the credits roll, OMAR *and* JOHNNY *are washing and splashing each other in the sink in the back room of the laundrette, both stripped to the waist. Music over this.*

END.